Tech Sales Wasabi

The Sales Engineer Manager's Guide to Hiring, Growing, and Managing Teams

Bill Balnave

Tech Sales Wasabi: The Sales Engineer Manager's Guide to Hiring, Growing, and Managing Teams

ISBN: 9798362158231

Cover design by Aaftab Sheikh, www.aafidesigns.com

Bill Balnave / billbalnave@gmail.com
7 Lebanon Gardens, London, SW18 1RQ, United Kingdom

About the Author

Bill Balnave has been involved in technical selling for over 20 years. He has worked in various roles for tech startups and large tech behemoths, including sales engineering, customer success, and product management. He has been an individual contributor, first-line manager, and senior leader. He has had the pain and joy of helping to build fast-growing, sales-focused SaaS companies. He has lived through multiple company acquisitions all while integrating new people and holding large teams together. The blend of roles and organizations has afforded him a unique perspective, taught some interesting lessons, and left some permanent scar tissue. This book is his first attempt at passing on some of the things he's learned to help the next generation of technical sales leaders avoid the same mistakes and achieve more success faster.

Table of Contents

Table of Figures

Forward

"I only wish I had this book fifteen years ago when I started my career in presales!" Those are the words I've heard people say about my book countless times. And they are precisely the words that I say now about this book – Tech Sales Wasabi: The Sales Engineer Manager's Guide to Hiring, Growing, and Managing Teams by Bill Balnave.

Like many SE leaders, I was a high-performing sales engineer looking for the next step in my career and moving into a management role seemed like the logical progression. And like many new SE leaders, I made the mistake of trying to be everything to everybody – a "Super SE" as I've heard it called. I experienced burn out and frustration. I alienated some of my people. And I learned through a lot of trial and error and some painful mistakes.

What I needed was someone to learn from. What I needed was a framework. What I needed was this book!

There are three reasons why I believe this book is going to become one of the most revered books in the presales industry: 1) the framework the book is based on, 2) the man who wrote the book, and 3) the manner in which the book was written.

Let's begin with the framework. It was defined to address an indisputable set of challenges that SE leaders face. (See Introduction.) The framework is easy to learn, remember, and apply. It's foundational. It's based on universal truths. And each of the practices is backed by scientific research AND real-life experience. It might not cover *everything* you need to do as an SE Leader, but it covers the MOST IMPORTANT things you need to do as an SE leader – to succeed, and more importantly, empower your team to succeed.

In Activate, Bill introduces a concept he refers to as the "SE Hierarchy of Needs". I consider this to be one of – if not THE – best thought pieces ever created in the area of presales leadership. In his words, sales engineers "have unique requirements to be able to grow and thrive". I'm anticipating that this *SE Hierarchy of Needs* will become one of the most frequently referenced pages in this book. It is the very foundation of what we as sales engineer leaders need to provide for the individuals – and teams – that we lead.

Next, if you're not familiar with the author, Bill Balnave, allow me to briefly introduce him to you. He's been in the sales engineering profession for decades. Like many of us, he was a technical expert prior to moving into presales. After a successful run as a high-performing SE moved into management. He's worked with large and small companies. He's inherited teams and has had to build them from scratch. He's learned as much from his failures as he has his successes. He's incredibly well-read and speaks – and writes – with passion and great insight.

And finally, the book… It's infinitely consumable. Bill writes the way he speaks, to the point where I can almost hear the words coming out of his mouth. And he's done his homework. His points of view are grounded in equal parts research and first-hand experience. Incidentally, he doesn't sugar coat things. In fact, some of his ideas may even seem controversial. This book is going to challenge you, challenge your thinking, make you think. In fact, you will likely not agree with everything he has to say. Nor should you! This book is as much about helping you discover the answers for yourself as it is about giving you the answers. But it does offer brilliant advice. In the book, Bill shares countless insights, and tangible, relatable stories that will make you a better SE manager and leader. Period. And a framework to guide you on the path to success.

If you are a new SE manager or leader – especially if you've recently been promoted from an individual contributor role – you have in your hand a gift of knowledge from Bill Balnave that is going to save you countless time and help you channel your energy in the best possible direction.

Even if you are a seasoned SE leader, this book is going to help you better "organize the tools in the toolbox", affirm and validate many of the things you're already doing, and is certain to give you some fresh ideas on how to succeed as a sales engineer leader in the post-COVID, modern era of presales.

Chris White
Founder and CEO of Tech Sales Advisors
Author of *The Six Habits of Highly Effective Sales Engineers*

1: Introduction

One of the hardest crops to raise as a farmer is Wasabi root. It only grows naturally in mountain stream beds in Japan. Since the 1980's, the rise in popularity of sushi in Western countries has increased the demand for Wasabi. Big time. This demand quickly outstripped the amount the natural ecosystem could produce. Japanese farmers had to figure out how to recreate the conditions under which they could get the Wasabi plants to grow.

But it wasn't easy.

Wasabi is a very particular life form. It's extremely sensitive to temperature. Any environment where the temperature regularly falls below 7°C or above 22°C won't work, as the plants won't tolerate that. Wasabi requires a lot of moisture, but not too much. It won't grow in, say, a submerged field like rice or cranberries. The soil must be constantly moist, but not soggy. The plants also don't tolerate direct sunlight. Thus, the Japanese mountain forest stream beds are the perfect place. But there aren't enough of those kinds of areas to grow all the Wasabi that the world demands.

So, farmers found other places in which to create the environment. They enclosed areas to fully control the environment or chose parts of the world where they could be assured of the correct climate. They developed special irrigation systems to let water flow over the plants without the soil becoming soggy. They erected coverings to reduce sunlight. The plants get what they need without being exposed directly.

As you can imagine, this is a significant amount of work. On top of that, Wasabi farmers can sometimes spend years just finding viable seeds on the open market. If they don't already have what they need, the search is long. Once they have seeds and the right conditions, it takes 2 years for a Wasabi plant to mature so it can be harvested. All of this makes growing Wasabi a lot of time and effort.

Why go through all of this? Because when good Wasabi root is brought for sale, it makes the work worthwhile. Wasabi fetches a great price on the wholesale market. Restaurants will often pay up to $300 for a kilogram of it. Its more common cousin, Horseradish, which is often used as a substitute for Wasabi after a little coloring and flavoring is added, only costs about $5 per kilogram. And it's not like the real thing. While it may be a finicky plant, Wasabi's value completely overshadows its cost. As the saying goes, the juice is well worth the squeeze.

I believe sales engineers are the Wasabi of the sales profession, maybe even of business in general.

It's not my intention to make them sound like prima-donnas; like spoiled celebrities who can't perform unless they have tubs of only their color of candy in their dressing room. Just the opposite. Sales engineers tend not to have such egos or make unreasonable and silly demands. The people who take on the sales engineer role are a unique hybrid of technical knowledge, sales acumen, competitiveness, desire to achieve, and desire to be recognized. There is no sales engineer personality type. There isn't a single profile into which all good sales engineers fit. It's a broad spectrum. They have in them some of what makes a salesperson what they are, some of what makes a developer or "techie" what they are, a bit of performer and a bit of artist. This makes them incredibly unique individuals. As such, they have unique requirements to be able to grow and thrive.

Let me build the analogy. If we think of the level of sales intensity for a given company like growing temperature requirements, SEs need just enough intensity to keep them busy and feeling useful. If it is too little, they get bored and look someplace else. If it is too much, they'll push as hard as they can but then get burned out and move on. If we think of development and challenge as the moisture requirement, SEs need a steady flow of it. They don't want to be relegated to delivering the same demo day after day, but too much time in training or onboarding means they don't feel like they're being useful. Finally, think of management as the sunlight requirement. I don't know of an SE that likes to constantly be told what to do and how to do it. They are an independent breed. They like to work autonomously. What they want from their management is to have obstacles removed. They want access to the tools and people they need. They want to be shielded from what they perceive as the corporate bureaucracy, but they also want to make sure they get the recognition they deserve.

And happy, satisfied, useful SEs will deliver. In most technology businesses, revenue doesn't happen without an effective sales engineering team. Unicorn startups don't achieve their crazy growth rates without sales engineers creating and delivering demos, pulling late nights and weekends, getting on planes, and visiting prospects. Sure, those sales engineers put the effort in because they believe in the big future payout. But the only way to sustain that pace is to make sure the SE manager can build and keep the right environment that supports the SEs' needs.

The Challenges Facing an SE Manager

Just like with Wasabi farmers, this is not easy. There are challenges an SE manager faces to be successful.

Challenge 1: Work Environments Lack the Right Elements

One of the biggest challenges is that *most work environments lack the right elements for an SE team to thrive and grow.* Wasabi root does not grow just anywhere. If it could, it would not demand such a premium. In the same way, SEs cannot be effective and deliver revenue for tech companies in conditions that are far from optimal.

Sales engineers are usually remote workers. The SE team tends to be distributed all over the place. There are many benefits to having an SE in the same time zone and geography as your prospects. But that means most of them don't work where the rest of the company works - so they don't feel connected. And they may be the only person in the company in that location. If they're lucky, there is a sales rep or two. But that means little to no contact with their colleagues.

In addition to being spread out, SEs also tend to have a variety of "homes" - but not one that is truly their own. Most SEs belong to another organization. Thye are usually part of sales. I have also seen them part of customer success, professional services, or even reporting to the CTO. They are then further subdivided into geographical teams, potentially under different top-line leadership. As a result, it becomes difficult for the SE team to gain any sense of identity or connection.

When I took over the European SE team for a SaaS company late in my career, there was this lack of environment. The former manager had his own quota as well as responsibility to manage the team. He focused more time on himself then on managing and neglected the team. Morale was low. Performance was lackluster. The EMEA sales

VP felt that everyone on the team was good, they just needed a focused leader. A year into the role, performance and morale was marginally better. The sales VP let me know that, while he did not think I was doing a bad job, he had received comments from the SEs that they didn't much feel like a team. While I was spending time with the individuals, I did nothing to create a cohesive environment to bring the team together.

Challenge 2: There is No Standard Definition of Good

Another challenge SE Managers face is the lack of a standard definition for a good SE. Ask an SE manager what a good SE is, and they will most likely say someone who knows how to deliver a good demonstration, gets along well with the sales team, and has been part of closing big deals. Ask the sales team, and they may say someone who is willing to do whatever it takes to get a deal completed. While in theory this may seem sufficient, in practice it is not. Each person will have their own perspective on what a good demonstration is or what it means to get along. A definition of good is only useful if it is consistent and detailed. It requires more than nebulous concepts like doing good demos and having a good relationship with sales. It takes understanding at a more granular level what a good demo is, what it means to deliver a good demo; what having a good relationship with sales means, why it is beneficial, and how best to do it. Combine this clearer, more detailed description with data to measure these elements and it becomes a usable definition of "good." Without that definition, there is no way that a manager can bring about any needed course corrections that lead to improved results.

I feel like I have so many examples of this in my past that they all blend together in my memory. I do remember many times, in more than one organization where I was a manager, having to deal with amazing feedback one week and condemning feedback the next on the same SE. This is how the human brain works, as I will discuss later in the book. When something positive happens, everyone is good. When something negative happens, suddenly those same people aren't so good. The human brain can't be trusted to make objective judgements without a clear standard to use. Emotion will sabotage logic, making it impossible for a manager to help his team.

Challenge 3: Current Hiring Profiles Are Too Limited

SE managers will also at some point need to hire. It would seem simple and easy to pick the "best" SE on the team and find more of that type of person. That notion presents two hurdles. First, that profile includes a relatively small population of candidates. Finding them will be difficult. There will be fierce competition from other SE managers at related companies who are also looking to hire that same talent profile. The second hurdle is this: when you clone your best SE, the benefit and value from this added person are not, in fact, additive. The Law of Diminishing Returns takes effect, with a quickly flattening curve. Why? Because teams of the same profile SEs – clones - lack the ability to innovate. They all think the same way. They all approach problems and challenges the same way. When it's time to try something new to bring about improvement, they are not agile enough to quickly adjust. To use an old-fashioned cliché about animals in a bad circus, they are a herd of one-trick ponies.

There was a point in my management career where I hired several very experienced SEs at the same time, all with about the same profile. I was excited because the company I worked for was growing fast. I believed I had assembled an amazing team to support this growth. However, fast growth also means fast change. And the solution was conceptually new in the market. We were constantly iterating the message, the approach, the product – everything. This team of like-minded veterans struggled with the change. I ended up losing almost half of them in less than a year, either because they voluntarily quit or because they just couldn't keep up. It made me poignantly realize what Marshall Goldsmith meant when he said: "What got you here won't get you there."

Challenge 4: The SE Career Path is Very Limited

Companion to hiring is the need to develop people and move them along their career paths. But the obvious career path for an SE is short. Sure, there are potentially levels of sales engineer through which one can move – SE, Senior SE, Principal SE. Some organizations even have an SE Apprentice or Technical SE role as a starting point. Past that – there is SE Manager, then Director, and potentially VP. The path narrows very quickly and ends just as quickly. And it doesn't at all take into consideration the fact that because an SE is exposed to products, customers, and selling – they build a unique viewpoint and experience that can provide value in a host of other roles – and may end up being interested in transitioning to one of those roles at some point.

I've watched too much good talent walk out of companies because of this lack of career path. And I mean not just talented SEs, but talented people period. I believe sales engineers are much more than demo performers. There are many examples of people who start in technology as sales engineers and go on to become CEOs. Too many people discount the exposure an SE receives. I'm not suggesting that all SEs are future CEOs. But there is a wealth of business potential that goes untapped, much to the disappointment of many SEs and SE managers.

Challenge 5: There is No Overall SE Org Operating Model

There is also an important side to management that is often considered boring but is critical for the success of the SE organization. Because managers must deliver results by leading others, they don't often have a direct connection to the results themselves. The results produced by an individual contributor are clear. There is a direct connection between what they do and results. The distance is short.

For managers, that distance becomes greater. They influence, coach, and direct individual contributors to produce results. The direct contribution of managers is much more difficult to measure. There are many more levers to pull and actions to take to produce those results. How do they know what to do to produce more or better results without having some ability to measure the effects of all these potential actions?

I have myself been blindsided by this complication. Managing the SE team is easy when deals are closing, and quotas are achieved. But then the sales team misses a quarterly target. You believe your team has been doing the same things that achieved results in the past. Except, those things don't work anymore. You wonder why and start the uncomfortable process of trying to figure that out.

SE Managers are in this position because SE organizations in general lack a standard and useful operating model – a way to measure performance and predict outcomes so that managers can understand why results weren't achieved and what might need to be done to avoid that in the future. Most of the time, the SE team hums along doing fine. After a couple of failed quarters and an attempt to change things, SE managers find themselves quickly looking for another role to avoid the inevitable consequence.

If only there was a model or framework around which to manage, so they could know what to do and then act on it.

How To Grow Your Own Wasabi

This is the mission of Tech Sales Wasabi. In here are stories and practices to help an SE Manager find the right people, create the right conditions for them, lead them, grow them, and deliver results.

I will cover six practices. The activities described in each should become habitual in everything you do as an SE Manager. You should also personalize how you practice them. While I will suggest activities and relay stories about what worked and didn't work for me, you should find your own way of incorporating them into what you do. There is no single right way.

To make them easier to remember, the name of each of the concepts begins with the letter "A" and encapsulates the spirit and intention of the concept itself. They are:

1. **Actuate**: *to cause to act in a particular way; to motivate*. This is about you and your own development. You can't effectively develop your team if you can't develop yourself. Your credibility with your team depends on this.
2. **Activate**: *to make something or someone operative; to convert a substance into a reactive form*. This practice will focus on creating the best working environment to foster the success of the individuals who report to you. You'll create the fertile soil into which your Wasabi SEs can grow and thrive.
3. **Advance**: *to make or cause to make progress*. This practice helps you define what is good when it comes to your SE team, how to measure it, and what do you do to keep and improve it. This is the core of your overall operating model.
4. **Augment**: *to make something greater by adding to it*. When the need arises to hire, this practice will provide you with the guidance to find talent that will increase the effectiveness of your team, not just replicate what you already have. This practice helps you step back and consider a broader set of elements for SE candidates. Doing this will help you elevate the entire team by adding people with a more diverse set of skills, traits, and perspectives.
5. **Advocate**: *to publicly recommend or support*. The SE team is part of a larger organization, and as such needs to understand how to work in that ecosystem to both increase the value they

deliver and capacity to deliver through collaboration with other teams.

6. **Aspire**: *to direct one's hopes or ambitions towards achieving something*. Developing people is the highest calling of a manager. Many SEs typically have a large desire to grow in their role and achieve more, but it isn't always clear what that can be. A well-worn career path doesn't exist. This practice will help you to help them forge that career path and guide them along the way.

Each practice comes with unique aims, the principles on which they are founded, examples from my own career, and some suggested activities to help make the guidance practical. Combining the six practices together gives the SE Manager an operational playbook that helps with both leading and developing people and achieving the results the business needs.

2: Actuate

The word Actuate is a bit obscure, but I think it has a special significance to being an SE Manager. If being an SE Manager is a calling, *actualization is the work one does to realize their highest potential in that calling.*

There are several prominent psychologists in history that referred to the notion of self-actualization. German neurologist and psychiatrist Kurt Goldstein originally coined the phrase. He brought a holistic approach to biology and neurology in his book *The Organism* written in 1934. He defined self-actualization as the driving force that maximizes and decides the path of an individual. Perhaps the most famous is American psychologist Abraham Maslow, who was influenced by Goldstein. Maslow referred to self-actualization in his paper "A Theory of Human Motivation" published in the journal *Psychological Review* in 1943. Maslow states "What a man can be, he must be. This need we may call self-actualization." Maslow felt that every human being had in them the desire to realize their full potential.

People who become sales engineers have this need. It's one of the traits that makes them pursue the role. How important is it, then, for those who lead sales engineers themselves to have the need for self-actualization, to continuously strive to improve? I believe it's of utmost importance. If you don't understand how to improve yourself, how can you hope to help someone else improve? If you don't work to develop yourself on a regular basis, how do you expect others to take your lead in doing so for themselves? Your ability to manage and your *credibility* with those you manage depends on it.

So, the primary aim for this practice is to *continually develop yourself so that you can best develop your team*. Self-development is personal. There are many ways to do it. I would encourage you to try as many as you find and be open to different ideas. Then find a core set of activities that you do believe in. Have these form the foundation of your self-work.

Embrace the SE Manager Mindset

When I took my first management role, I was fortunate enough to work for a director who embraced the importance of people management. Rather than just leaving me to figure it out myself, he shared a wealth of guidance on how to properly start and establish myself in the role. One of the first things he told me was to get myself into a manager mindset. It sounds simple, but it's not necessarily a natural thing for an SE to do.

Most SE Managers were once exceptionally good SEs, which is why they were promoted. But what made them great SEs doesn't translate into making them great SE Managers. SEs typically like to please their sales counterparts. When an SE provides a successful demo or is part of the team that closes the deal, there is a fair amount of recognition they'll receive from the sales team and the salespeople with whom they work directly especially. SEs work independently. They don't need to interact with the other SEs unless they need help. This combination of enjoying the spotlight, pleasing sales, receiving tons of recognition, and doing your own thing works directly in opposition to the mindset and behaviors you need to have to be an effective manager.

One of the most important things you do when you decide to manage others is to *step out of the spotlight and push your people into it*. It's your job to stop thinking about the recognition you'll get and start looking for ways to get your people recognized. This can be challenging because many first line SE managers are expected to be "player/coaches." They're asked to do all the work their SEs can. They will be called upon to deliver on those special occasions – say, in front of the prospect's executive team – because they want someone with a title. Their credibility will also depend on how well they present the solution in the field. The sales team will expect them to know as much or more than the SEs do; otherwise, their ability to influence and help them is thought to be limited.

Which makes it easy to be pulled "back into the field." An account executive calls you because he scheduled a presentation with an important prospect, but the sales engineer he normally works with has a conflict. It's simple to step into the opportunity yourself versus finding a good but less utilized SE to who to give the opportunity. Suddenly that same account executive needs you again. Each time it becomes more difficult to refuse. You can easily find yourself doing as many meetings as the people who work for you. Or you find yourself leading the most important ones. This will cause resentment among your team, and you'll start to lose them. It takes regular, conscious effort to take your ego out of it and ensure you tip the scale of spotlight time toward your SEs.

Also, realize that while you're pushing your team into the spotlight, you're in a different spotlight of your own. You should be aware that not only will your team be watching your every move and listening to your every word, but so will the sales team, business development reps, Regional Sales Managers, and... well, everyone in the company. Now that you have the title, the expectations of you instantly change. Do your best to be positive but truthful. Think two or three times before you say anything. Make sure that you believe in what you say and can defend it. Don't take part in discussions just to be right or show you're in charge. Be super careful about what you say about others. In fact, better not to say anything at all. I would tell you I still sometimes get pulled into conversations like this, and I only regret it afterward. The high road is the best place to be. It will make a huge positive impact on your ability to lead your team and their confidence in you. Your team will be examining what you say about others and assume that you will say the same things about them. Make them proud to have you as their boss.

Third, and for me this was the hardest to internalize, have patience. *Great management should be boring and uneventful.* For an SE, customer meetings should be mind-blowing and mountain top experiences. For an SE Manager, most of your meetings will be about building relationships with your direct reports, reviewing the forecast, updating your team, and following process. These are not mountain top experiences, nor should they be. Don't try to make every one of these meetings have an intense emotional impact. You will do better for your team and yourself if you realize that the value of these meetings comes over time, and not in an instance. Your impact happens in the day-to-day stability and consistency you supply your team and the business. And when the mountain top moment does come, make sure the spotlight shines not on you but your direct reports and all who contributed. Go into your office, shut your door, and give a couple of fist pumps. Then on to the next thing.

Know Where Your Time Goes

One of the most important things to do to actualize yourself is manage your time well. Time is the most valuable resource you have, and the one resource over which you should exert the most control. Many do not believe this statement. They fill their diary with every meeting to which they're invited. Their online calendar looks like a lost game of Tetris. They believe that the organization owns their time because they're in management now. That they have no choice. They relinquish control to the others around them – their direct reports, customers, other managers, and the executives in the company. They may also believe that agreeing to as many of these invitations as possible is a demonstration of how good they are. I'm sure you've heard the litany of the "self-important" manager: *I'm back-to-back. I'm double booked. Evenings are the only time I do actual work. I don't have time for my day job.*

I used to recite such things myself and see others nod in understanding and awe. Of course, this is the way of the manager. You're so important that you must respond to every email and attend every meeting to which you're invited. I came to learn that this is the opposite of what a good manager does, and the opposite of what the organization needs.

The fact is you DO have a choice. There will be obligatory meetings you must attend. Those are the meetings typically scheduled by your boss or top-line executive that have some statement about being mandatory in the title or description. There are some that are supremely important for you to attend, as you can't be effective in your role if you don't. The meetings in these two categories make up a minority of the total meetings to which you are invited. The rest of the meetings you attend at your discretion – or better yet, delegate to someone on your team to whom you want to give more responsibility. You may also feel that being invited means you're considered important. I would suggest that it's not your importance that drives the invitation, but the desire of the inviter to be as inclusive as possible.

Managing means being in charge. It means being able to make effective decisions about how best to guide people and use resources to grow and operate your business. Time is the most important resource you have. If you can't effectively manage it, how can you expect to manage a team or a project to produce an outcome?

When you invest your money, the expectation is you'll increase the overall amount of money you have. You may have put many hours into choosing those investments and then checking their progress to ensure they are positive. Or you may have even hired experts to ensure your success. If you realize a loss, you know you can work again to make more money. Ironically, most people do not put the same amount of effort into managing their time. Which is a finite resource. Once you've spent it, it can never be recovered. This is no account that allows you to add more time to your life. How much more important it is, then, to manage it wisely.

Where You Should Spend Your Time

It's impossible to manage time moment by moment. You can easily become overwhelmed with considering all the potential things you can be doing. It helps then to decide where your time SHOULD go. Consider categories of the things you can do and prioritize those. I think about those categories this way:

1. Time to develop yourself
2. Time to develop and manage your team
3. Time to work on growing revenue directly
4. Time for other asks of the organization

You may consider my suggested order to be controversial. If managing is about other people, why would I prioritize self-development first?

I am not suggesting that you consume as much time for yourself as possible and give everyone else the remaining. In fact, if you consider a percentage distribution of your time for the week across these four categories, your top priority doesn't receive the most time. It just means that you do it first to ensure it gets on the calendar, not squeeze it in between meetings and customer calls. Most people I know do this first thing in the morning, before generally-accepted working hours. If you have global responsibility, I realize that's every hour. Just schedule as best you can.

I'm also not suggesting that you never move your self-development time. I wouldn't tell my boss or a sales RVP that I couldn't attend a meeting because it conflicted with my journal time or my workout. What I would do is find an alternate time to journal or workout and make sure that I did it.

This is where the challenge is and the difference. When it comes to choosing between spending an hour reading or meeting up with your colleagues for happy hour, it's a tough choice. You tell yourself that time with your colleagues is important. And it is, but not if you consistently sacrifice your own self-development to do it. This is the real meaning of putting your self-development first.

Guiding and motivating your team is next. Now this is the category that should get most of your time. It includes your regular one-on-one meetings, team meetings, and any coaching and development you do with your teams, either individually or in a group. It also includes the effort spent thinking about and preparing for these activities.

Since the other half of being a manager is results and you are part of sales, customers need to come next. Just like the first category, you should purposefully make time to be on sales calls or in customer meetings. I believe this is especially important for a manager of sales engineers. You need to be able to understand what the selling environment is like and the challenges your team faces. You'll get this by attending meetings with them. But you will understand it better when you do the role like they do. Yes, I know I said this is about them being in the spotlight not you. And that you should not get dragged back into the field. And you shouldn't. If you are purposeful about what you get involved in, you should be able to balance your customer facing time with making sure your team gets more of it.

What's left you give to the rest of the organization. There will be many activities that fall into each of these categories. The trick will then be organizing yourself so that the way you invest (not spend) your time aligns with these priorities. This is also how you know which meetings to accept, which to delegate, and which to decline.

There is an analogy that I think best highlights how to achieve this. It's extremely popular, so I'm sure you've heard it. I'll confess I don't know the origins. The story goes that a philosophy professor shows his class an empty jar. He then places as many larger rocks as he can into the jar and asks the class if the jar is full. When they indicate that they believe it is, he then adds pebbles until he can add no more. He asks the same question – to which the class replies in the affirmative. He then pours sand into the jar until he can't. You get it at this point. The rocks, pebbles, and sand all stand for the activities you do, by their priority. Rocks are the most important, pebbles the next important, then sand. In your case, the rocks represent you; the pebbles your team; the sand is customers – and then there are atomic size activities that represent the rest of the organization. *Adding things into the jar in this order is the only way to get everything into the jar*. The same is true of your diary. The only way you'll have time for everything you need to do is if you start by setting aside time for yourself first, then the activities you need to do for your team, then what you need to do for customers, then for the rest of the organization.

I suggest you schedule as many of these activities as you can. I used to write out my activities on a prioritized list but not put them in my diary. As a result, what I intended to do and what I really did were two different things. *It wasn't until I put the activities in my diary that what I did with my time started to align with my stated priorities.* I would also constantly update my diary based on any changes I made. It's near impossible as an SE manager to set a plan for the week and then follow it as originally set. You'll need tremendous flexibility. Sometimes you need to dump out the jar completely, rearrange the large rocks, then put the pebbles and sand back in. Or sometimes you need the pebbles or sand in a certain spot. If you update, you'll then have a historical record to be able to assess if you're keeping aligned with what's important. That way you'll know if you need to adjust.

Focusing on Self Development

Your approach to self-development – the big rocks – is personal. There exists an incredible number of resources in the form of books, websites, blogs, consultants, and services. There are many methodologies and practices. Because this is such an individual activity, find what works best for you and practice it. At the end of the book, there is a section titled "Bibliography of Readings That Inspired This Book." You'll find some of my favorite self-development and leadership books here.

Developing yourself is a continuous practice. Your commitment to it will determine how much benefit you receive from it. It's not at all static. It will need to change as you change and grow. What initially benefits you may not continue to do so. Mental development is like physical development. Professional athletes know that you can only use a given workout and diet plan for a limited period. The body adjusts, and the regime no longer gives the same benefits. Only when you surprise the body with a new diet and workout do you then begin to realize the benefits again. This applies to all aspects of self-development. While you can't keep doing the same things and get the same results, there are categories of activities that always have benefits. Within each, practicing a variety will ensure continued value. They are:

Reading

This is the core of continuous learning. Read some non-fiction every day. I also suggest books should make up a majority of what you read. While there is goodness in blogs or articles you find online, I've benefitted most from reading entire books. I also live by the belief that I only need to take away one idea or a single inspiration for a book to be beneficial. And the inspiration may not be directly related to what I'm reading, but a thought inspired based on it.

Journaling

This practice can help you get to know yourself better than anything else you do. What I refer to here is not keeping a log of your activities or a history of your life. I use my journal as a place to have a dialog with myself. It's the one place where I have learned to be completely and totally honest with myself. By doing that, I see my situation and who I am with more clarity. By acknowledging my true thoughts and feelings, I liberate myself from their potential negative effect on me. I can pull myself out of an emotional downturn or find the motivation I didn't think I had. I also notice the difference when I go for periods of time when I don't journal. I'm less motivated, more stressed, and more affected emotionally by external factors. Journaling is a great way to keep the belief in yourself and your ability.

Meditation

Starting the morning with 10-15 minutes of quiet can be extremely energizing. During that time, I focus on counting my breaths. As my head starts to spin with all the things that need to be done that day, I acknowledge those thoughts and let them go. I try not to dwell on them. If I start to feel anxious, I'll pick a part of my body and focus on relaxing it as completely as I can. Then another part and continue until I reduce the anxious feelings. All while continuing the count. At first, it's easy to follow a thought and lose your place. As you practice, you'll come to realize how counting can clear away that noise and help you focus on a single thing.

Morning Routine

Establish a morning routine – a set of practices you follow every morning. Mine consists of the above 3 activities, which I try to do every morning before the world starts up around me. I get a clear head, energized self, and a sense of accomplishment when I can which positively affects the rest of my day. And the opposite is also true. I find the day more difficult if I don't start with my routine. I encourage you to find a routine of your own that supplies the same benefit.

Stay Current

This is especially important for an SE Manager. Technology changes at an ever-increasing rate. Highly likely, the product you sell is enhanced at a similar rate. The internet makes keeping up much easier, as you can configure alerts to push information to you, rather than having to search it out yourself. This isn't something you need to do daily. Setting aside some time (1-2 hours) on a weekly basis should be enough investment. You should focus on keeping current in your industry, on your competitors, and on your own product. It's also worth suggesting your team do the same. In addition, it may help to ask a different person from the team to update the rest of the team on what they've learned, on a regular basis.

Measuring your Self Improvement

Whatever self-development activities you decide to do won't matter unless you know you're getting real benefit from them. The way you measure that benefit is very subjective. Throughout the book, I'll encourage you to use data as often as you can to measure progress and improvement. That is still possible with self-development, but you'll only understand your progress when you first really understand who you are right now.

Which means assessing your current state. Most leadership books discuss characteristics that make up a good leader, things like empathy, patience, curiosity, gratefulness, and authenticity. There is also the notion of what good for each of these looks like. In other words, what behaviors show that a leader has these qualities.

You can use this to track the progress of your self-development. First name those characteristics that you want to have as an SE Manager and more importantly as a person. For each of those characteristics, describe in as much detail as you can what you think it means to live by them. Put that aside for a day or two. Then, take some time to honestly assess how well you think you match those descriptions. This becomes the foundation for understanding those areas you want to improve.

As you look at the gaps you have between your ideal and how you are now, think about the things you can do to make progress. Make these the areas that you write about when you journal, the subjects of your self-dialog. You may quickly find that your initial self-assessment doesn't really align with how you are. This is progress itself, as you are now getting to know yourself better. Continuing to review this list on a regular basis and making notes about how your behavior in these areas has changed will help you keep this self-development work at the front of your mind, and that awareness will permeate the other aspects of your life.

The other way to track progress in self-development is to simply see how often you really do the activities you've decided to pursue. I call this a Habit Journal. I've built mine in a spreadsheet. Each column stands for a day of the week, each row stands for a self-development habit I want to practice (reading, meditation, journaling, etc.) At the end of each day, I put an "x" in the cell for that day that corresponds to the activity I completed. I set monthly goals for the minimum number of days I want to have completed the activity. As time goes by, I notice the more difficult weeks and months are those with the least amount of self-development activities in them. The journal reminds me of the importance and motivates me by wanting to check the boxes every day. While it's basic empirical data, it acts to motivate and keep me focused on the development and improvements I want to make.

Conclusion

In answering the call to be an SE Manager, you've also accepted the responsibility of working to realize your full potential. It's exceedingly difficult for you to be of use to your team, your customers, and your organization if you are not first effective with yourself. Practicing Actuate means putting self-development first. It's about investing time and effort in improving yourself so that you have something to offer those who work for you, your customers, and the larger company of which you're a part.

3: Activate

Most corporate environments are not tuned for sales engineers. For that matter, most SEs don't find themselves in the corporate environment. What I mean by "tuned" is this: the entire work environment, not just physical facilities, should fulfill the needs of the people in the role. It should be accepting of the common personality traits of this collective group of people, and even encourage them.

As an example, I've seen software companies go to great lengths to accommodate the working habits and personalities of those who write code. Rather than put people individually in cubes, they place their atomic teams in rooms with moving desks, whiteboards, and refrigerators. They supply 2-3 monitors, allow the person to choose their brand of mouse and keyboard and chair. They encourage a high degree of personalization. They adjust the working process itself so there are daily "stand-up" meetings, which offers people who are normally introverted to connect and speak. It gives those people a chance to be recognized and encouraged. There is an understanding that such social interaction can be difficult, so there is understanding and patience. As a result, the software company gets the best efforts of these people as well as their loyalty. The environment is tuned to the personality and work habits of the programmer.

I've seen this kind of attention given to the SE team once in my career. The software company had many branch offices in US cities, but I didn't live in one of them. Fortunately, there were several employees in the area, so we had several rooms in a shared office space – a nice one. One my first day, the manager at the shared office greeted me and brought me to the room that was mine. There was a box waiting for me that held two laptops, network cables, and LAN hub, and a projector. An ACTUAL PROJECTOR. The laptops were pre-configured with my accounts and connections to all the relevant supporting software. An envelope in the box held a document that walked me through final setup steps. On top of this, throughout my time at the company, there were other elements tuned to the SE team. Product marketing regularly came into the field and included the SEs in planning and decision making. Customer support had a special group that supported SEs working a customer proof of concept. We were even encouraged to call the development teams when we needed something for a deal or had feedback from a customer. And this was not a small SE organization. This was an environment that had truly been **Activated** for the SE team.

Activate means to make something or someone operative; to put them into action. Wasabi root doesn't grow unless activated by the right combination of temperature, moisture, sunlight, and nutrients.

The goal of Activate is to *create and maintain a work environment purposefully designed for sales engineers in which they can thrive and grow.* The SE Manager does this by

- Naming the key elements of that environment (what does an SE need most?)

- Understanding how to foster those elements in the organization to which they belong
- Implementing programs and activities to make that environment a reality.

This is normally not a tall order. With the SE team it's complicated not just by the physical dispersion but also by the fact that HR and other groups in the office don't typically understand enough about SEs and what the team does. I remember being caught off guard once when the head of financial planning asked me to speak to his team. He was trying to give them more information on different roles in the business so they could better support the annual budgeting process. There were a lot of questions about why the SEs were even necessary and what they did that was different from the salespeople. This event made it noticeably clear to me just how isolated we were from the rest of the company, and how isolated my team must have felt.

I realized then that creating this environment falls to the SE Manager. The manager can't do it alone, but it is up to him to lead and coordinate the work. There are a set of needs that apply to every SE and ways to accommodate those needs so that it is possible to create an environment in which the SE team thrives, whether that team is in the office, remote, or both.

The SE Hierarchy of Needs

I referred to Abraham Maslow earlier as the foundation for the Actuate practice. Self-actualization, his notion of ultimate human achievement, is really the last step in an overall *Hierarchy of Needs*. His theory goes that there are a set of needs that all humans have. Humans are then motivated based on which need they need. Maslow proposed that the needs build on each other. The first of those needs is the physiological – air, water, food, clothing, shelter, sleep. Without filling them, a human being can't function. Once a human feels some confidence that they can regularly fill this need, their focus shifts to the next set of needs and is their prime motivation. After physiological, Maslow proposed that a human is motivated by the need for safety. This is safety in every aspect of the word, not just physical but emotional and financial as well. Next a human is motivated by the desire to belong to something bigger than themselves. They want to be part of a family, have friends, and know intimacy, acceptance, and trust. Next, a human looks to gain esteem (sense of self), to fill cognitive needs (ability to think and create), to achieve aesthetic needs (beauty in self and the world around them), until finally that human realizes self-actualization. While these needs are met in this order, one set of needs does not need to be completely met before a human would look to fulfill the next set. As such, these ideas have been used in many different sectors and evolved over the years, but the model is the same.

To create the best working environment, the SE Manager must help each SE meet their needs. Maslow's hierarchy provides a great framework to use, with each need building on the previous one. By progressively meeting these needs, an SE Manager can help SEs realize their full potential. Though Maslow did not originally arrange the needs in a pyramid, it's the visual that has become popular and one that I will use as well.

Here is my take on the SE Hierarch of Needs:

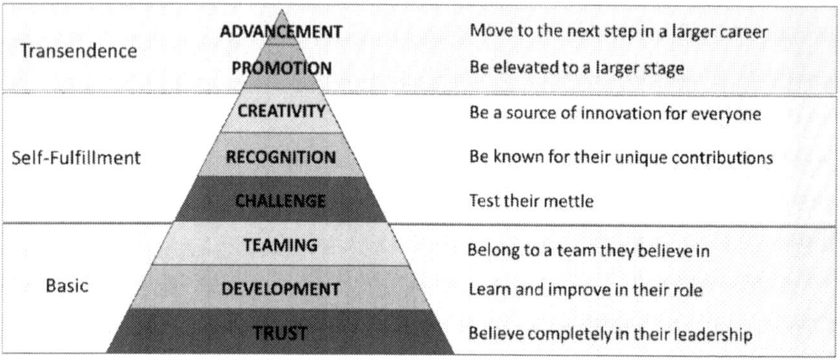

Figure 1: The SE Hierarchy of Needs

The base of the Hierarchy is *Trust*. This is more than just the natural trust that occurs between people. SEs tend to be more sensitive than the average person and even more fragile. They are often very protective of themselves. Unless they feel that their manager has their best interest at heart and puts them first, they will do what's necessary but won't put much faith in anything else.

Why does this happen? SEs tend to lack trust. Part of what makes them successful is that they question things and want to prove it for themselves. In addition, they perceive SE Managers as "management" and not really SEs. They assume managers will put the company's needs or sales needs before theirs. Not addressing this belief swiftly leads to low morale, poor productivity, and high attrition. The exact opposite of an Activated environment. As such, focusing on building and keeping trust should be an SE Manager's highest priority.

Once a certain level of trust is achieved, the SEs will be open to more from their manager. What they typically want next is Development. They want to continually learn and grow in their role. The blend of high achiever and competitor as major personality traits forms the basis for this need. SEs want their manager and the organization to offer them full support in this development. They want to learn new technology and products, improve their ability to present, and have what they need to grow not just in their role but also into the next one.

As they feel they are being developed, they also want to become part of something bigger than just themselves. SEs can do their jobs without anyone else on the SE team. They will spend more time with sales and customers than the people on their own team. But they crave the sense of stability and satisfaction that comes from being something bigger. Sales or the company is too big. And they want to huddle with "their own." So Teaming is the next need.

Challenge comes after that. It's the way in which an SE tests their mettle. As they achieve the confidence that comes both from development and being part of the team, they are ready to stretch. SEs want to know that not only can they use what they've learned but that they can amplify and extend it as well. They became SEs in some cases because they didn't want the predictable day to day of programming or financial reporting or data analysis. They wanted to face constantly changing situations that force them to figure things out or work differently than they have in the past. SE Managers need to challenge their SEs regularly, either by the sales situations in which they find themselves or through other activities.

The other side of the Challenge need is Recognition. Many believe that people become SEs because they like the compensation – the ability to earn more based on sales performance. But this also means the SE enjoys being recognized for their success. They don't want the paycheck without the spotlight. But recognition for sales performance comes at most 4 times a year. SEs need much more than this. And that recognition needs to have meaning. Recognition given just to give it or based on revenue alone has almost the opposite effect. They want to be recognized for applying themselves in a difficult challenge based on something they did individually and not working with an AE.

As an SE improves their abilities in the job, they want to be able to bring some of themselves into it. They want to feel that their expertise is appreciated and respected. This is the need to use their Creativity. SEs want to channel their expertise into creating something new to the company. SE managers need to actively find those kinds of outlets for them.

In addition to Recognition, an SE wants to be Promoted. This is not necessarily a job promotion, although that is certainly one way. The Promotion need is one where an SE's abilities are put in the spotlight for the rest of the company or world to see. This promotion gains that SE the opportunity to work on a cross-departmental project, be part of a company initiative, or take another role. It's the SE Manager's job to find the right forum and shine that spotlight.

Finally, they will start to look past the SE team and their individual role to be something greater. The first form of this is the opportunity to work in a bigger arena, perform on a bigger stage. I call this Promotion. This could be presenting in front of the entire company at an all-hands meeting, presenting at an analyst conference, contributing to regular social media posts that use their product and industry knowledge. And for some SEs, this point is their self-actualization. They don't seek anything further from the role or even their career.

But other SEs will want to continue – and that means Advancement out of the role into management or another part of the business.

These needs build on each other. It's not necessary to fulfill one need to begin the next. In fact, it's fair to say that there is continuous work on each need and a minimum level of fulfillment that should be achieved. The SE Manager should regularly examine how well each of these needs are met for every individual. Everyone on the team will be on in a different part of the pyramid. It's important not to think of meeting the needs of "the team" but of each member of the team.

Building Trust

I believe it's fair to say hundreds of books exist about building trust in relationships; and thousands of articles and assorted social media posts. There is a tremendous amount of wisdom about it in the world provided by people much smarter than me. I will not try to recreate any of that here. But I believe this is a crucial element of Activating the work environment, so I'll focus on the activity an SE

Manager should do to build and keep trust and what indicators to look for to know they have it. There are five precepts to follow.

Be Consistent and Reliable

Much of someone's trust is based on knowing that something or someone will be there *every time* they're expected to be there. According to Oxford Languages and Google, the definition of *consistent* is "acting or done in the same way over time, especially so as to be fair and accurate." From that same source, the definition of reliable is "consistently good in quality or performance; able to be trusted." When thinking of these two words used together it can mean having superior quality and performance by doing the same thing continuously over time.

While this may seem boring or obvious, it's crucial to making an SE Manager effective. You meet when you say you're going to meet – week after week, month after month, quarter over quarter. You give the help or programs or outcomes you say you're going to every time; and if you can't, you're quick and thorough about why. Consistency and reliability take time to prove. The Trust need can't be filled without them. SE Managers must have the patience needed to deliver the same good stuff over time to create the consistency and reliability that Trust needs.

The practical guidance here then is to do things that help you prove both. Conduct regular team meetings. Don't worry so much about whether the agenda is lively and interesting. Instead, make sure you conduct them. You will find that for the meeting that you don't have planned topics, some amazing discussions will happen. Conduct one-on-one meetings with each of your direct reports every week. When conflicts arise, move the one-on-one meeting rather than cancel it. Allow your SEs to talk about whatever they want in that one-on-one. Make it their meeting, not yours. If you have topics to discuss, schedule a separate meeting unless your direct gives you permission to use the one-on-one. For the most part, I follow the one-on-one meeting guidance provided by an organization called Manager Tools (https://www.manager-tools.com). I found it to be the best trust-building activity in my time. And finally, respond back to your SEs first, before you respond to a customer, sales manager, or your boss. Over time, they will come to see your consistency and reliability and develop the belief in you needed for you to effectively begin to Activate the work environment.

Be Communicative

Building Trust through communication isn't just having your team hear from you. It's about what they hear. It's about you become a source of information about the region, the company, and even the industry. The director I worked for in my first management role was exceptionally good at this. He kept himself informed on the industry and our competition. He stayed connected to other leaders in the company. Very often I heard about what was going on from him in a team meeting or one-on-one. It inspired tremendous confidence and trust.

It does require that the SE Manager develop an awareness to listen to what's important to your team and get it to them as quickly as possible. It's better if the team hears about a new hire or someone leaving from you vs. a general email sent to a large distribution list. They should hear about a change to the business – new product, new marketing campaign, new messaging – from you as often as is possible vs. reading it in a press release. This also means you may need to actively pursue the information rather than passively wait for it.

You won't always be the first source. Doing this as often as you can builds their confidence that you are highly engaged in the company and your role. It gives your position credibility, which in turn fulfills that Trust need.

Be Vulnerable

Some believe that being a good manager means always appearing confident, positive, poised, and having everything in order. Displaying emotion or having a life outside of the work environment isn't something good managers do. But they should, especially when you lead SEs. SEs want to know that their manager is human. They need to know that you'll be understanding of their individual situations. They want to be able to confide in their manager. They want to see that their manager will not put the deal above everything else, including family and friends. That their manager will be compassionate, looking out for their best interests first and not the best interest of the company or the deal.

Vulnerable is when a manager shares that they're having a tough day, or that they are distracted by a personal matter. Vulnerable is when the manager shares family stories with. Vulnerable means the manager reveals who he is as a person, so they can see he is not just management.

Be Protective

SEs can sometimes find themselves in precarious positions. The sales team will have unrealistic expectations and make requests that aren't practical. The company may make a mandate that for most employees isn't difficult but may be more complicated to follow for an SE. The SE Manager must do his best to protect his SEs from these types of things, or at least champion their perspective to upper management.

While this may not often be a concern, it will come up. You'll receive a call from a sales manager who is relaying to you some negative feedback from a sales rep about a demonstration one your SEs performed. They'll expect you to do something about it, despite that SE having no idea about this sentiment. It would be easy to relay the feedback to the SE as is and ask him to do better next time. Many new managers might even feel obligated to do this. You'll build Trust if, instead, you first attempt to understand the situation better by contacting the salesperson directly, hearing from them, and then contacting the SE to see how they felt the demo went prior to relaying any of the negative feedback. In many cases, connecting these dots will reveal that there wasn't really an issue, or it was something minor. It will also give you the ability to connect the salesperson and SE so that they can develop the kind of relationship that allows them to give feedback to each other directly.

Never ask your SEs to do something you wouldn't. Never assume something about them without first asking and understanding fully. And shield them from any unnecessary negativity or bureaucracy. When the SE team knows you have their back, you will meet their Trust need.

Learn Each SE's Preferences

Technically, an SE Manager can't build trust with a *Team*. It would certainly make it easy if that were the case. The manager would need only worry about one entity, understanding and meeting the needs of that single entity. But that is not the reality.

Team is just the logical name given to stand for a group of people – individuals. Building trust with a team means building trust individually with every person on the team. And each person is different, with different personality, traits, and preferences. To build trust with every individual requires learning everyone's personality, traits, and preferences.

This prospect may seem overwhelming. First consider that this isn't something that happens instantly or even quickly. If you think about any long-term friend you have, you may still find yourself learning something about new them even after knowing them for years. This is how relationships develop naturally. There is no shortcut to this process, but there is a way to be more purposeful about it.

Create and use an individual profile document. This profile would contain a set of elements and categories so that you can record and have on hand the preferences and personality traits of each of your direct reports. As you spend time with them through your normal interactions, use the profile document to recall what you know about each one and what you need to learn.

I have successfully used the E3 Leadership Profile from a firm called E Equals Why (https://eequalswhy.com). The form associated with the profile supplies a framework of the things I should discover about each individual and then a place to record it so I can recall it. During a one-on-one or team meeting, I would have every SE's profile open. When I had the chance, it would give me suggestions of things to find out. As I learned, I would record it in the profile.

There isn't necessarily a right way to do this, but here are some suggested categories and elements to use in your profile doc. Some of these things you can learn by asking directly. In other cases, you'll infer them based on conversation and observation.

Demographics
Languages
Schooling
Marital Status
Number of Children
Parents Still Living
Places Visited
Hobbies

Motivators
Travel Preference
Recognition Preference
Ideal job
What activities excite the most? Least?
Money vs. Recognition

Personality Traits
Openness
Extraversion
Agreeableness
Conscientiousness
Emotional

Preferences
Morning routine
Problem-solving
Decision Making
Communication
Working Style
Feedback
Learning

You may be tempted to create a form or survey and ask your team to fill it out – to speed the process. While you may get the information back faster, what you won't get is the relationship building that happens when you gather the information over time, which is as important as getting the information itself.

Gathering the information is the first step. Once you have it, you need to put it into practice. Some of these are easy and natural to incorporate. For example, you'll quickly notice how a given individual prefers to communicate – whether it's email, phone call, text message, or Slack. You'll know based on the communication channel they respond to quickest and most often. In other cases, you'll learn over time. It may take several 1-1 and team meetings for you to learn a given individual is very introverted. This means that while they may have an opinion and wish to voice it, they may not always be comfortable doing so. You have the opportunity as their manager to find ways to invite them to offer up their feedback in a safe group setting so they feel they have a voice.

By connecting with people in the way they want and being aware of what motivates them and how they work, you prove to each person that you care and respect them. There is no greater way to build Trust in an individual than by connecting with them in the way they want to connect.

Developing Your Team

Developing people means more than training them. It's not just about what they know or what they're capable of doing, but who they are. One of the reasons people become sales engineers is because they want to do something bigger than what they were doing. They aspire to be more than just a programmer, more than just a sales rep. They want to use all their talents and do something that is more than just a job.

When a good friend first told me about this role called sales engineer, I'll admit I was a big confused. I had the worst impression of who salespeople were: money driven soulless people without principles who would take advantage of anyone they could. And engineers were introverted, anti-social people completely consumed by the desire to figure something out and rebuild it. Why would I want to be a combination of those two types? What I learned was extremely far from that. I found a role that allowed me to take advantage of both my ability to learn and adapt quickly, my good communication skills, my desire to perform, and my love of the spotlight. It was the combination I thought I would never find and did. And once I had it, I wanted to ensure that I took full advantage of it.

I believe this is what most people learn when they discover the sales engineer role. They are grateful and excited. In their excitement, they push to be the best they can be. Like the musician who, upon first picking up an instrument, doesn't want to put it down. Or the athlete who constantly practice for simple love of the game. The role is precious to them, and they want to be the best they can be because they love it so much.

And SEs know they need help. But because the role is so important to them, they won't get that help from just anyone. Therefore, gaining trust first is so important. Once SEs believe in their manager, they will place their development and progression into that manager's hands.

Unfortunately, most organizations do not have a dedicated SE enablement team. It falls to the SEs and SE leadership to decide how to develop and the tools and collateral to use to drive that development. In thinking about this situation, I am reminded of an old proverb: *"As iron sharpens iron, so one person sharpens another."*[1] So while there may not be a separate team to help

[1] Bible, New International Version, Proverbs 27:17

develop the SEs, the best development can come from the SEs themselves, organized by their management.

Every SE manager should create and manage a specific program that supplies regular enablement of the entire SE team. They should look to their senior and most tenured SEs to help deliver it. They should seek the help of other parts of the organization – product management, engineering, product marketing, support – to provide material and perspective. It is a big job but an extremely important one. It isn't something that happens very quickly, so SE managers need to develop a discipline and long-term focus to continually make progress with SE development. And as it turns out, this is the best way to fill this development need for your team.

Connecting Your Team

Trust and Development are individually focused. The manager builds trust with each SE. Every SE has different development needs based on their experience and tenure. While these are foundational needs, they do nothing to address that gap in the work environment that leaves SEs feeling like they are on their own.

Recall my story from the introduction of the time I took over an existing SE team that its former manager neglected. For a year, I focused on trust and development. At the time I thought these were the two things on which to focus to ensure the team received the attention it needed. I was wrong. The other thing missing was the fact that the team didn't feel like a team at all. They felt no sense of connection to each other or anything that unified them together as the EMEA SE team. They were better connected to the individual sales reps and other people in their geography. I scheduled a recurring team meeting, but also regularly cancelled it because of conflicts. And because everyone on the team had some tenure, I thought they would appreciate having the time back. I was completely wrong. They wanted that time together – even if there wasn't a set agenda or some critical topic. They didn't consider it yet another wasted meeting. Once I learned this, I made sure to keep the meeting in place. And it didn't take long before I could see a marked difference in everyone's attitude, simply by having a way to connect with the other SEs weekly.

The lesson I took away from this was two-fold. First, SEs want to be part of a team. Second, it takes purposeful effort on the part of the manager to bring that team together. Left on their own, the SEs may make some one-to-one connections with other SEs. It's the manager's job to bring them altogether regularly. And it's more than just weekly team meetings or quarterly outings at a QBR meeting. I suggest you help make a deeper connection.

In one of my later roles, I lead both the sales engineers and customer success managers for North America. While it sounds grand, it was a small but remarkably diverse team. Some of them were brand new. Some had been with the company for 6 or more years. They had never really collaborated with each other and up until I joined were not part of the same organizational team. While conducting regular team meetings was a great start, I took the advice of friend and mentor Kathy Eastwood, founder of E Equals Why. I hired her to moderate an exercise that involved each team member presenting information about themselves and then brainstorming together to build a team mission statement. As part of this, we all took the Clarity 4D™ survey to reveal our color profiles, and then shared those profiles with the team. The entire exercise lasted several weeks and cemented a connection I found remarkable. It had an incredible effect on everyone, who all separately remarked to me how valuable they found it.

Creating a sense of team is as important as building trust and developing each SE. It requires purposeful effort but pays back in big dividends.

Challenge

As SEs gain new knowledge and skills, they want to put them to the test. This is the need for Challenge. It goes beyond just the baseline test of knowledge or using the knowledge or skill in a live customer situation. SEs want to know they can apply it when it really counts. There was a famous American TV show called MacGyver in which the lead character is a genius with superb engineering skills and knowledge of physics. Every week he would find himself trapped in some way. He would then use his abilities to cobble together ordinary items he found around him to create some ingenious device that allowed him to escape. Every SE wants to be MacGyver. They want to find themselves in some situation where a prospect puts them to the test so they can take what they know and apply it in some new way.

You want this for your team as well. However, those prospect facing opportunities don't always appear promptly. In addition, you want to see the SE in action in a low-risk scenario prior to having them face a customer. To fill the need, create programs that can address both the ability to offer the challenge to the SE and the ability to have them perform in a low risk setting before it counts.

There are several ways to do this. My favorite is something I call the SE Game Show. Choose a well-known game show format (Jeopardy, Wheel of Fortune, Family Feud, are a few I've used. Find whatever works for you). Create questions or other content that aligns to a particular aspect of the being an SE or some knowledge related to the industry or product. You can also typically find an app or website that will allow you to automate the game with your own content. The SEs won't really need and special preparation for this activity, other than to know it's coming. It can help to gamify, so set it up to be able to award points and celebrate a winner.

One version of this I've used successfully I call the Wheel of Objections. Objective handling is an area that is regularly updated and refined with experience, new product capability, and new competitors. The Wheel of Objections gives the SEs a chance to get the best from each other and improve how they all manage prospect objections.

To play, find a configurable online spinning wheel. Add to it as many of the objections you would like to highlight. Let each member of the team have a spin. When the wheel stops on a given objection, they have 1 minute to decide how to respond. Award 1 point for a pure verbal response, 2 points if they include a useful slide, and 3 if they use the product to respond. I also added a twist. After the SE that spun finished their response, I opened it up to the rest of the team – to the first one or two who offered to supply a better answer. If another SE's answer was, in fact, better, they were able "steal" the points from the original SE that spun.

While some may believe that the competitive nature of this activity could discourage those who don't win, I have not ever experienced that. All SEs know that succeeding in sales means winning deals, and that they probably won't win every deal in which they're involved. It's important to learn how to properly deal with both situations. The tone you set as the manager also makes a big difference. Keeping focus on the positive and not being concerned with any potentially negative performance will create a better atmosphere.

Whatever the activity, combine elements of fun, competition, and creativity, and keep the feedback and tone positive. This will help fill the Challenge need in the team.

Recognition

Recognition is an SE prime motivator. While some SEs consider themselves motivated by the chance for large bonuses or commissions, all SEs love recognition for their performance and ability.

Most SE recognition is based on their involvement in a big sale or successful quarter. Sales leadership decides and provides it. This recognition is important but limited. It awards for a single achievement – sales performance. Something for which an SE has influence but not control. *It ignores the other behaviors and activities that make SEs great, and that SE leadership should encourage.*

A recognition program for sales engineers from sales engineer leadership is a useful way to fill the Recognition need. Such a program should once a quarter supply a physical award (trophy, plaque, something similar) to the SE that in that quarter did something other than work on the biggest deal. I recommend the SE leadership team choose the recipient unanimously at their discretion. In some cases, and based on team size, there may be a reason award more than one person.

There are some guidelines to ensure the program has the intended impact. First, the program should award non-deal related activity or behavior. This is a chance to award someone on the team for something they contributed that helped the whole team or had an impact to some other team in the organization. By recognizing in this way, it highlights and reinforces the things you want the entire team to do. Second, the size of the recipient pool needs to be large enough that the award matters and isn't simply being passed around between the same 4-5 people quarter over quarter. If there aren't at least eight people on a team, then this program isn't useful. It may then make sense to consider the entire global team, not just a region. This would mean regional leadership collaborating and agreeing on the recipient. Third, present the award in front of the entire team by the recipient's direct manager. In addition, announcing it to the entire sales organization or company via email also adds impact to the award.

Creativity

At some point, as SEs gain confidence in their ability and experience many different selling scenarios, they develop a perspective on how to improve that selling experience. They want to have their input considered and even adopted by the rest of the team if it proves itself. They also have ideas based on years of interactions with prospects and customers on how the product could be enhanced, or products that could added to address what they perceive as unfilled needs. This is the Creativity need, which surfaces in varying degrees in SEs. In some cases, they'll come to you with suggestions. In others, they may take it upon themselves to try them out or even present them to product marketing or sales.

SE Managers should look to fulfill this need as directly as possible. Demonstrating the company's solution is clearly a primary responsibility of the SE team. Developing the messaging and steps for solution demonstrations is also ultimately up to the SE team. For those SEs who have the right depth of experience, the opportunity to help create new solution messaging and demonstrations fills this Creativity need.

One programmatic way to do this is something I call the Demo Throwdown. This is an exercise intended to simulate prospect-facing conditions but encourage creativity. To conduct the exercise, create a scenario designed to put the SEs into specific customer challenges or product capability. The narrower and more focused the scenario, the better. Fashion it as much as possible against a real-life selling situation. Along with the scenario, create a scoring sheet awarding points based what you want the content and style of a demo for this scenario to be. Review the scenario with the team but not the scoring sheet. Give them 2-3 weeks to prepare. The scenario should require only a short demo to fulfill. Then gather the team to watch each SE deliver their version of a demonstration.

Give points based on the scoring sheet and then announce point totals and a winner at the end.

There are more considerations for this activity. Don't hold the event during a busy time for the team. Because it will require effort to prepare, you don't want this to seem a burden. When you give feedback during the event, it's important to emphasize only the positive aspects of each person's demonstration. This is NOT a demo coaching session. The aim is to encourage them to be creative and take risks. You need a perceived safe environment to do that. Also, be open to giving points for content or style you consider creative and didn't expect. By having everyone take part, each SE will typically learn something from the others' presentations. By keeping it positive, you give everyone an injection of morale and confidence and encourage them to think past the standard demo content.

In other cases, the SE Manager can indirectly help fill this need. The SE team is typically the voice of the solution to its prospects and customers. They are also a bi-directional means of communication, as they bring back feedback about the solution to the internal product and engineering teams. And while the SE Manager can't control what the product or engineering team does with the feedback, it can create the conduit for the SEs to communicate it.

I have a suggestion to help with this: the Field Advisory Board. Do this in conjunction with the products and engineering team. Have representatives from the SE team meet with Products and share what they've learned in the earlier period. In turn, ask the products team to share the plans they are making for the product in the coming quarter and seek the input from the SE representatives. It's a lightweight activity and can involve a different set of SE representatives every quarter. SE Managers can use it as a potential reward, but it adds a venue for an SE to express their creative ideas about the product.

Promotion

This need isn't about a career path, but instead follows the definition "activity that promotes or encourages a cause, venture, or aim." Each of the SEs that works for you wants to be your cause, to be promoted to their fellow SEs and to the larger organization around them. This is not about recognizing the individual but about giving them opportunities to have a broader impact outside of what SEs normally do. There aren't necessarily specific programs to fill this need. This instead requires the SE Manager to actively network within and outside the sales organization to find projects, activities, and events for which an SE would be suited based on their skills, experience, and talents. This might be something like presenting at an analyst overview session or providing a demo with the CEO at an executive briefing session for a marquee customer. These events are typically rare, and the SE team isn't necessarily at the top of the list to take part in them. This takes some active investigation by the SE Management team to bring it about. We'll spend more time with this later in Advocate.

In addition, many SEs get to the point where expertise in their solution and experience working with prospects and customers is valuable for more than selling. In many cases, these SEs have insights and leadership at the industry level. SEs that get to this point are motivated by opportunities to share what they know in non-sales venues. This may be at conferences, user groups, or other forums that involve communicating solution insight and industry best practices. Certainly, the most immediate possibility is the other side of the Development need and using these SEs to enable and train the rest of the SE team. Other opportunities to fill this need include leading a session at the company's user conference, speaking at an analyst conference, leading a webinar, or delivering training or best practice sessions for customers. SE Managers should actively seek out the opportunities and Promote their expert SEs as good candidates.

Note that for some SEs, this is the top of their needs pyramid – their self-actualization. They want to remain on the SE team but contribute in as large a way as possible. This is a good thing. People should be able to make an entire career as a sales engineer without having to move to another role. Good SE Managers know how to meet the ever-changing needs of those SEs.

Advancement

And then some sales engineers will wish to progress their careers into different roles. The most obvious of those is either management or sales. Whatever that happens to be, I've dedicated an entire practice to this need (Aspire). I think this could be one of those places where sales engineers are most underserved. Many SEs develop amazing business minds because of the different parts of the business to which they're exposed in this role. But because their CV reads "sales engineer," they often considered for more than this.

Conclusion

SEs are a hybrid of different personality types and characteristics. Because of this, they require a unique work environment in which to thrive – an environment that meets the SE Hierarchy of Needs. It's the responsibility of SE leadership to create and support such an environment. It starts by you building and keeping Trust, instilling in each SE the belief that you put them first and have their best interests at heart. This is best accomplished by learning how to communicate to each individual SE based on their personality and preferences. From there, you activate the remaining needs by implementing programs and activities to help and by finding the right opportunities within the organization.

4: Advance

All business functions use metrics to measure how well they're doing. For a metric to be useful, a few things need to be clear. First, the business should know how the value of that metric should change over time. With Sales, revenue is the most important metric, and it should always increase. Next, the business needs to understand what actions should be taken to cause that metric to change the way it should. Sales needs to understand how the activities and behaviors of the sales team help revenue to increase period over period. This is where things get tricky. If revenue didn't improve quarter over quarter, what went wrong? Is it the wrong salespeople? Is it the sales messaging? Are salespeople pursuing the wrong types of prospects? If it did improve, was what the sales reps did in that quarter make it happen or was it just luck?

To answer these questions more definitively, other metrics associated to revenue and activity can help connect sales activity and the revenue achieved. Most sales organizations use a sales process with defined stages. They look at various metrics like conversion rates between stages and average deal times and break them down by region or product or business line to discover patterns, then follow the patterns that are associated to success.

This is basic logic. Hopefully, it doesn't insult your intelligence. It just still surprises me that often this data collection and metric analysis does not include anything related to what the SE team does. And many SE organizations don't bother to collect data for themselves at all. They leave themselves to the whim of pure sales metrics to measure their success. The problem with this is that there is too much distance between what the SEs do and the outcome that the metric measures. For example, it's nearly impossible to measure how often a demo leads to a closed deal. There is too much time and too many activities that happen between the demo and the time the deal closes to feel confident in the correlation. But this is often what is being suggested as a good measure SE effectiveness.

In addition, rather than metrics, sales and SE management may rely on people's opinions as a measure of performance. This puts the SE team in a risky position. If opinion and feelings are the measure, how does the SE team respond if that performance is questioned? What can the SE team do when people are suddenly asking about the value the team brings to the sales process and to the company? These questions may seem farfetched, but there are sales engineer managers who are currently being asked these questions right now. And they find themselves with that sinking feeling of not knowing the answers.

Advance means to make or cause progress; to move forward in a purposeful way. There are three ideas in this simple definition that are important to consider. First, there is the implied intent to progress. That means movement. For some organizations, keeping the current state is sufficient and sometimes preferred. This is not usually true with SEs. They always want to progress – learn more, sell more.

Next, progress also implies moving forward. To move forward, there must be two points: where the organization is and where it wants to go. Which means that moving in other directions is not desired.

Finally, there is the question of being able to understand what needs to happen to cause the organization to move in the intended direction. To do this requires a way to measure this progress. I may know where the organization is and where I want it to go, but if I can't track its movement, there is no way to know if it will get there.

Therefore, you need metrics to manage the performance and quantify the value of the sales engineer team. The aim of Advance is *to continually assess and develop the team using metrics to drive top performance AND communicate business value.*

Both are important. Don't assume that because you measure the performance of the team means that the rest of the company understands its value. You also must communicate it. Otherwise, it is the proverbial tree falling in the woods. If no one is there to hear it, it doesn't really matter whether it makes a sound or not. The event is irrelevant.

For this practice, you first must decide on the metrics to measure and get a regular data source for those metrics. You then need to understand how to use those metrics to influence performance, forecast added headcount, and justify the need for more training or supporting resources. The vehicle for much of what you do in Advance is a Sale Engineer dashboard or control panel. It doesn't have to be sophisticated, and it shouldn't require significant effort to create and support. Function is vastly more important than form, usefulness over size or volume.

What Is Good?

It seems like a simple question, but it has no simple or easy answer. When people pose the question about Sales Engineers, the all-too-often answer I hear is: "I'll know it when I see it." If you consider the person answering this way to be an expert on SE performance, that may be acceptable. The issue is that the definition of "good" is based on how this person *feels* about the SE and not on anything standard. A presentation or demonstration is a complicated event. There is a lot that happens - a complex set of information to consider when thinking about whether an SE's performance is good or not. The problem with relying on feeling is that the brain is lazy. Relying on someone's opinion may give you one view of how the SE did, but it isn't consistent and doesn't help you figure out what to make better over time.

In his book *Thinking, Fast and Slow*, Dr. Daniel Kahneman talks about using expert intuition. His Noble Prize-winning work reveals the risk of relying on such judgment:

"Another reason for the inferiority of expert judgment is that humans are incorrigibly inconsistent in making summary judgements or complex information. When asked to evaluate the same information twice, they often give different answers. The extent of the inconsistency is often a matter of real concern."

He goes on later in the book to say: "Remember this rule: intuition cannot be trusted in the absence of stable regularities in the environment." Anyone who has spent any time in technical sales would suggest that there are rarely any "stable regularities" when it comes to convincing people to buy.

This leads me to suggest the **Intuition Principle**: Using gut feel and intuition to figure out the quality of your team and their abilities are at best problematic. Therefore, *the use of data and standard measurements is essential.*

Be a Service Provider

To answer the question of what to measure and how, I will apply a paradigm used extensively in financial companies and IT organizations.

Managing performance and delivering outcomes are the basic operational processes of a business. In the end, if a business entity can't deliver it's intended outcomes it fails. It can't predict if it will deliver those outcomes, it can't manage its performance.

When I joined the IT organization at Ford Motor Company in 1989, its leadership had the notion that IT should treat everyone else in the business as if they were our customer. After all, the people in IT didn't build cars. We existed to help make it easier for the people that did build cars to do their job. In a way, it's like we were an IT *services* company inside of Ford. We provided people with automation technology: PCs, personal productivity software, applications, network, storage, and printing so that their jobs were easier and cheaper to do. That way they could build more cars for less cost. This notion wasn't unique to Ford, either. It was soon a movement in most IT organizations inside of lots of other companies.

As this movement progressed, it also expanded. External IT Service providers appeared and claimed they could deliver the same IT services cheaper than what an internal IT organization could do. Now CIOs had to not only supply the IT Services, but they also had to measure the cost to deliver them and the quality of those services as they were compared to what an external service company could provide. CIOs found themselves running a business inside of a business. They had to put process and data collection in place to understand their performance and communicate their value to the rest of the business – and in some cases compete for their job. There were situations where entire IT organizations inside large companies were let go or moved to an external provider to supply those services for less. The IT organizations that stayed intact learned how to measure their performance and communicate their value.

To be clear, I do NOT think that sales engineers are at risk to be outsourced. But I do believe that if the SE Team were to think of sales as its customer, think about the activities it performs as services, and measure the quality and performance of those services as if it were a business inside of a business, this forms the foundation and focus to drive the right improvement. This is a great framework to ensure the SE team can Advance.

Using the Service Provider Framework

Let's examine how this might work.

An internal service provider belongs to and is embedded within an individual business unit. It is tightly coupled with the internal customer. There is no competition. It has intimate knowledge of the business itself: goals, plans, and operations. It is highly specialized for that business unit, designed to support its specific needs. Its growth is controlled by the growth of the business unit to which it belongs.

If sales is the business unit, is it not fair to say that the sales engineer team fits this description very well? I want to emphasize that I'm suggesting this as a framework and mindset. I'm not suggesting that the SE team should look to cross-charge sales for its services or think of itself as subservient to sales. To my understanding, there are some sales organizations that have suggested it and even tried it. This extreme approach undermines the partnership that should bond the AE and SE team. What I am suggesting is you apply the parts of the analogy that are useful to you in advancing SE performance. Here is how I think that application could go.

Service Delivery

The basics of the framework follow the circular process you see below. While there are six steps, it's not intended to be heavy or require a ton of administration. In fact, I would suggest it's how you think about managing what you do, but not something you publish or advertise. You need only as much process as necessary to add value. Start basic and add more only when it becomes necessary or helps you better manage the team.

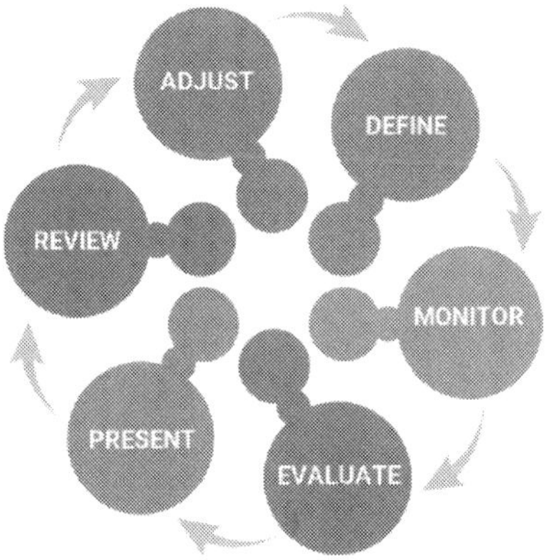

Figure 2: Service Delivery Framework

Define

First *Define* what you do for sales. It would be easy to shrug and assume you already know. You're doing it already.

Most sales and SE leaders take for granted what the SE team does: RFP responses, demos, POC activity, run trials, answer technical questions. Use this list to answer two questions:

"Is this really all we're doing?"

"Are these the things we SHOULD be doing?"

There will be many things you do for sales one-off. No need to list those. There may also be some things you list but don't do enough of to worry about measuring. At one SaaS company for whom I led presales, we probably responded to less than 10 RFPs per year. We weren't selling to organizations who bought that way. While we did them, there was no need for me to invest any time thinking about are performance related to them or how to improve that performance. It just wasn't worth it.

In thinking about what to measure, you should have for each a:

1. Definable outcome or deliverable.
2. Clear understanding about the people and resources needed to deliver the service
3. Metric that describes the quality and performance of what you're doing, with the understanding that affecting that metric affects quality and performance in some predictable way.

So now let's go back to that list of things you'll rattle off the top of your head:

- Responding to Requests for Information or Proposal (RFP/RFI)
- Conducting Discovery meetings
- Demonstrating the solution
- Conducting Proofs of Concept and / or Product Trials
- Providing technical overview presentations

For each of these, I'm sure you can articulate the three points quickly. Here is how I might characterize these for completing RFP responses:

<u>Writing Responses for RFPs/RFIs</u>

Desired Outcome or Deliverable:	• The completed RFP/RFI document • Acceptance into the evaluation process
Required People and Resources:	• Sales engineer assigned to the opportunity • Potentially others from products, services, customer success, legal • Past RFP responses • Current lockout documents
Quality and Performance Measure:	• Percent of time your response gets you selected to move forward in the process

How to Use Service Definitions

While you may never use it outside of the context of the SE Team, thinking about them this way makes it possible to use a consistent method to understand what the SE team should be doing and how to measure it. Take it a step further by keeping track of who in the SE team can deliver on these services and who isn't ready to yet. Doing this gives you the most basic understanding of your team's capacity, and where you should spend time in enablement.

This helped me in the early days at a fast growth startup. There were multiple modules to the platform, some requiring specific industry knowledge to understand. Most SE activity was either demonstrating product or delivering a proof of concept (POC). There was typically a first meeting to help understand a potential customer's pain and current situation, which always included a demo. Given that we sold to IT organizations, there was a wide range of potential problems to solve and applicability for our software. It was difficult to expect an SE to understand everything to the degree to which they needed.

I created the SE Capability Matrix, which functioned as my Service Catalog. Rather than just 3 services – Discovery, Demo, POC – I listed out services by module. I knew not every SE could deliver a demo or POC around each module, and many didn't have the domain knowledge to even ask the right questions or understand the answers a prospect gave. I kept track for each module what an SE was able to demonstrate and for which he could deliver a proof of concept. Every quarter, I worked to fill in blank spaces through enablement and shadowing. The Capability Matrix also allowed me to compare what sales was asking for vs. what I was able to do. It revealed that there was more to supporting a sales cycle then just demonstrating "the product." As a result, I was able to get support for additional headcount and funds for the outside training needed to properly deliver on these services and close deals. (We will visit the Capability Matrix again in Aspire).

Monitor

Once you have defined what you do, it's time to understand how well you do it. This means *Monitoring* - tracking both how often and how well you deliver. This is the heart of understanding if you're doing the right things for this business and where you may need to make improvements.

Some of you will immediately bristle and think to yourselves: "He's talking about time tracking." It always fascinates me how most SE leaders immediately jump to that conclusion. They then tell tales of how they attempted it, and how the data was worthless, and it made all the SEs angry and want to quit. There is a TON in there on which to comment – and I'll get to all of it. But let me first declare unequivocally that I am in no way talking about time tracking. I am one of those SE leaders who was part of an organization that asked their SEs to account for their time. The effort was not worth the benefit. Most SEs felt they needed to pad the number of hours they recorded. They were concerned this data was being used to track if they were working enough. And anyone without enough hours would be at the top of the list to let go when the next workforce reduction came. Not only was the data useless, but it also made the SE team paranoid.

What I AM suggesting you track is all customer facing activity in which an SE participates. It's a simple matter of gathering this basic information:

- Name of the prospect or customer
- Type of activity (presentation, demo, POC)
- Which SE delivered it
- The date on which it happened.

Truthfully, this is probably all you will ever need. It is easy to collect and easy to validate. Leverage the existing CRM system, if the SE team has access to it. By putting some remarkably simple standards around data entry in place, this is something every SE should be able to complete no more than 30 minutes at the end of each week. It also removes the paranoia SEs have accounting for hours and has them focus on what's important: working with the sales team to deliver services to close deals.

Now you have visibility into what types of services your team delivers and how often. It's also helpful to collect anecdotal information through interaction with both the SE and sales team. It is something every SE leader should do regularly. It doesn't need to be done for every customer event or even necessarily related to a specific event. It should be as simple as an email or live conversation with an AE or SE – or preferably both together. Ask two questions: what is working well and resonating with the prospect, and what isn't. Then take this information and review it in combination with the data you're collecting. This is how you'll begin to associate data with what's happening in the field.

Evaluate

Evaluate was for me the fun part: pulling the data together to see what I could learn. Most SE managers don't really know how to do that. Truth be told, most managers don't know either. If you have never done data analysis, I suggest you find a book or two to help with the basics. I am no data scientist, but you won't need that level of sophistication. Here are the basics that have served me well.

First realize that having data is the beginning of the analysis, not the end. It drives the questions but doesn't necessarily supply the answers. It's not useful to attempt to draw conclusions or make decisions just looking at numbers. The numbers by themselves don't really mean anything.

The first question you need to ask is this: How complete and accurate is this data? And you need to accept that it will never be 100% complete and accurate. That is normal and acceptable. "Perfect" has been the enemy of good data analysis too many times. Don't let it stop you. Good enough is all you ever need.

What is "good enough?" That of course depends on the questions you want to answer. In our case, we want to know if we're doing the right things and how well we're doing them. To answer this, we want to know:

- How often our SE Team's activities lead to revenue
- Which of those activities do and which don't (generally)
- How much of those activities do we need to do to win business.

Your "good enough" data is having most of those activities recorded. And just like you're asking each of your SEs to record their activity at the end of the week, you should be reviewing that data to confirm it at the beginning of the next week.

I would regularly review a basic report I created in the CRM system that showed activity count by type and SE. I would then visually review SE calendars to see if the counts aligned close enough to the meetings I saw. If there was disparity, I would follow up with the individuals in question to make sure they updated the CRM system. In addition, I would use my knowledge of the deals in progress to confirm meeting types. For example, it wouldn't make sense to see discovery meeting recorded after the POC had occurred. I would follow up with that SE to ensure they had recorded the correct meeting type. Despite what you may think, this really wasn't time consuming. I blocked off my calendar for 30 minutes on Monday morning to do this or reviewed it while I was on a Monday flight.

Now the objection I typically get is that this is a form of micro-management. I will tell you - most definitely - it is not. This is called management. It is the manager's job to determine how SEs spend their time. I always told my SEs: My job is to determine where to spend your time, your job is to execute to the best of your ability. Validating how they spend their time is the only way you'll be able to determine if you're doing the right things at the right time in the sales cycle.

Now you may ask: at what data should I be looking? Where do I start? My suggestion is that you look at the long pole in the tent. Decide which service the SE team does that requires the most effort, is the riskiest, and is the most important activity in a sales cycle and evaluate it. As examples, I remember in my first year at a startup, we had an awful first meeting to active deal conversion rate. But once we convinced a prospect to evaluate, we did well. Despite it being early in the sales cycle, this was the long pole. Focusing on the first meeting demo became priority, and it was something I analyzed monthly. In another situation, we could get a prospect to the point where they agreed to a POC, but then the POC would take sometimes months to complete, and our success rate was unacceptable. So, this was the focus of my data collection and analysis.

Wherever you start, I suggest you start slowly – just a few data points at a time. It's tempting to grab as much data as you can and create lots of tables, graphs, and charts. But having too much to look at becomes confusing. The story of what's happening with the team is lost in the noise generated by all the data.

Whatever your starting point, make sure you use *relative* data points, not absolutes. *Context is everything*. Looking at how many times you performed an activity is meaningless. Understanding how often that activity led to the deal progressing or achieving the technical win tells you something. Informing sales or product management that you delivered 20 POCs in a quarter doesn't mean much. Is that too many? Not enough? Did we do well? Instead, *look at the percent of time a POC leads to a technical win*. This means you'll be combing more than one piece of raw data into your contextual data point. In this case, you'll need to see the total count of POCs for a given period. For each POC, you'll need to see whether the prospect awarded you the technical win in that deal. That will give you the number of POCs that contributed to a technical win. Now divide the two to obtain the percentage.

In addition to determining a small set of initial data points, you should also set a goal or threshold for each one. This makes them a true Key Performance Indicator - or KPI. I've heard the term metric and KPI used to mean a broad range of things or used interchangeably. They should not be. A metric, in business terms, is a quantitative value with a unit attached to it. Like 10 demos. Think of a KPI as a metric with more useful information attached to it – namely, a desired threshold and a trend indicator. There is a value and unit you want to maintain, and a trend to indicate if you're getting closer or further away from that desired value.

Here are some suggested initial data points:

Percent of POCs that lead to Technical Win: As described above, this is calculated by dividing the number of POCs associated to winning deals by all POCs from a given time. The higher the better. Given the effort required in a POC, you should target at least 70% as a desired overall threshold. This KPI makes the most sense to review at the end of each quarter but aggregating for the whole year. Don't look at the quarter by itself. The trend will tell you if you're getting better at POC execution.

Percent of time The First SE Delivered Demo leads to an active sales cycle: This is dependent on how you track a sales cycle and when the SE gets involved in it. This will be a bit more complicated to calculate, as your first demo may happen in various stages of the sales cycle. Which may be the KPI to track first – at what stage is a first demo delivered. For a given period, group the count of first demos delivered by the sales stage in which they were delivered. Further break that down by deals that progressed past that stage. You'll first be able to answer how effective your demo is (did the deal progress) and when is the best time to deliver that first demo. Looking at the Percent of time First Demos lead to an active sale tells you whether you are demoing too early AND whether your messaging is effective. This should also be a high percentage – certainly greater than 50%. If it's not, you're using the SE's demo too soon and not doing enough discovery to determine if you're a good fit for that prospect's needs.

Number of Demos per Sales Cycle: For this KPI, you should look only at sales cycles that are complete – meaning won, lost, or marked dead. This metric should be an average based on data you continue to accumulate, which is total number of demos performed for complete deals divided by the number of those deals. Break it down by deal outcome as well. This will tell you how hard you need to work vs. how effective your demos are. It may be that you'll need to do 3-4 demos for different audiences. Or one gets it done. Either way, this will help you understand what capacity you need to execute a deal. Sales will typically look at their overall number, average deal size, and win rate to back into the number of deals required to make quota. You can use that same logic and this KPI to determine how may demos you'll need to do, and how many SEs it will take to do it.

Percent of RFP response that lead to selection: This metric is like the POC Technical Win metric. Figure out the total number of RFPs to which you responded in a period. Determine the number for which you were selected to continue. Do the division, and that gives you your percentage. I would look at this both on a quarterly basis and overall to see if there are trends.

Regarding RFPs – I've always believed that if you didn't help the prospect create the RFP or know that it was coming before it was issued, you're probably not their first choice. I think many have different ideas about whether they should respond to an RFP or not. This metric will answer some of that question. Every industry and situation are different. You know you're most likely going to respond anyway, as this is what sales will want.

Use your base set of KPIs over the period of 2-3 quarters before you add more. The underlying objective of all of this is to be able to associate data with behavior. You need to have some confidence that you understand what the data tells you about the impact of your team's activity, so you know that a change you make could truly have its desired effect. It will first take you time to determine that. One quarter isn't enough to confidently make the association. You'll also come to realize which KPIs have more impact than others. It may not matter how many demos you average in a sales cycle if most of the time you do a POC you don't get the technical win.

Use the data to know which questions to ask. Just like when doing discovery with a prospect, keep asking why until you have a complete understanding. If your percentage of POCs leading to the Technical Win is low, then you need to ask things like: What are the characteristics of deals where we do get the technical win? Are they long POCs or short POCs? How involved is the prospect? Is it the same when we don't? Pretend you're sitting in the QBR with the head of sales and CEO. What would they ask you? What would they want to know? Whatever you can't get from the data, make sure you're asking your SE team to provide the details. This leads me to the next way of measuring performance.

Using an Objective Standard

You should establish an objective standard for delivery of each of the services. KPIs will help you know if you're getting the results you need. These standards will help you define what you need to do to achieve those results. My suggestion is you leverage a framework known as a *rubric*. A rubric is a scoring guide that describes performance expectations for an activity. It is a table with two dimensions: the criteria to be measured and the description of various levels of quality for each component. Part of a rubric for a solution demonstration might look like this:

Demo Element	Setup	Presentation Style
Definition	Steps the SE takes to prepare the prospect for the demonstration and align the demo to the prospects needs.	*The effectiveness of the SE's communication style and ability to make a connection with the prospect and adjust the way they present based on prospect reaction.*
Needs Improvement	SE provides an introduction but does not describe the flow of the presentation or the capabilities that will be demonstrated. SE does not ensure that all prospects have identified themselves.	SE speaks either too quickly or slowly making them hard to follow; voice has little to no emotional expression; SE in general uses too many words to explain what they're doing; when in person, SE uses little to no body movements or gestures; SE makes no effort to connect with the prospect and continues through the demo without refering to specific prospect members by name or role; SE rarely pauses to ask for questions or confirm understanding.
Adequate	SE asks the prospect to introduce themselves and explain their role if this has not already been done. SE introduces himself/herself and provides some relevant background to establish credibility. SE then provides an explanation of what will be shown and summarizes the flow of the demonstration, including what products will be used and the capability that will be validated.	SE speaks at an appropriate pace; articulates words appropriately; when in person, makes eye contact and uses hand gestures to emphasize a point or create an emotional impact; when remote, faces the camera to appear to speak with the prospect and doesn't just look at their screen or keyboard; sometimes adds the right amount of flair and enthusiasm to highlight an important point; makes a regular verbal connection to the prospect throughout the demo by pointing out relevant capabilities to the right people; pauses appropriately to confirm the prospect's understanding and solicit questions; refers to prospect members by name or role at points in the demo that are relevant to that prospect member
Exceptional	SE uses a relevant Disruptive Truth at the beginning of the demo to capture attention. SE introduces himself/herself and provides some relevant background to establish credibility. SE explains what will be demonstrated with relevant detail using the prospect's terms. SE also queries the prospect to confirm their individual interests and discover if there is anything else not previously mentioned. SE then either makes the appropriate adjustment in the demo or indicates that additional topics may require another meeting.	SE varies tone and speaking pace to provide emphasis on important points; SE projects an emotional belief and conviction about the solution and its value; when live, makes regular eye contact with multiple people in the room and does not stay in one position but moves to provide interest but not a distraction; when remote, SE positions the video feed to ensure they are facing the prospect as often as possible and appear to be looking at them; SE pauses appropriately to confirm understanding and ask questions; SE refers to prospect members by name; SE refers back to prospect-specific needs / desires stated at the beginning of the demo and points out areas that would be of interest to the prospect member based on role

Figure 3: Part of a Demo Rubric

I’ve transposed the table, so it fits the page better. In this example, the first row contains the different parts of a demonstration. Each column then represents a different part of the demo to evaluate. The next row defines that that part of the demo is. The remaining rows provide a detailed description of the levels of quality, in this case Needs Improvement, Exceptional, and Adequate. Publishing rubrics for each of your services makes clear to your SE Team what the performance expectations are and gives you a means to give objective feedback to how each SE performs.

I would suggest that demo and POC are the services for which a rubric is mandatory. Discovery is a close second. To make this useful, I also suggest you develop it in collaboration with your team and sales leadership. This will give your team a sense of ownership and give sales a say in how they want their services delivered. You should also update it as you gather feedback on what works and what doesn't.

Present

Communication is a critical part of this process – but doesn't happen unless prompted. I was one of those SE managers who at first didn't really offer anything unless I was asked. And I would wonder why I wasn't being asked. Wasn't my SE team a critical part of the selling process? Why wasn't I invited to speak at quarterly sales review meetings?

This may lead you to believe that the sales team isn't really that interested. And *that's true if you don't have anything interesting to offer them*. Giving them charts and graphs, or just providing metrics and KPIs is mildly interesting at best. More likely it seems complicated and distracting. The sales team is interested in how you can help make them successful. So, you need to present your data and analysis so that they clearly understand that.

This first step is to assemble what you're measuring into some format that your audience can easily consume. It should be simple and succinct. Don't waste a lot of time creating aesthetically pleasing dashboards with lots of creative visualizations on them. You'll get lots of compliments, but the usefulness will stop there. I remember a visit to a major financial institution in the UK that was a customer. They wanted to know how we could help them automate and improve the monthly business reports that their CIO used to manage the IT organization. Technology is extremely important to a financial institution – it IS their business. I expected a very sophisticated, online, interactive business intelligence platform with the latest in smart visualizations. What they showed was a PowerPoint deck with five slides. Just five. There was one column chart in the entire deck. The rest of the report was tables with numbers and text. All black and white. The first slide had five metrics on it and nothing else. As they walked me through how they used this PowerPoint deck to successfully guide the IT organization every month, I realized the uselessness of those visually dense colorful dashboards. I used to think that I was the one that was missing something and needed to learn how to read them. Turns out simpler is better.

Throughout my time in leadership, I followed this practice of basic reports, summarized, in PowerPoint, with numbers and tables. I used data extracts and Excel, then pulled the important information into PowerPoint to present. I was consistent, quarter over quarter, with a base set of metrics. I would then add commentary that was relevant to that time as text on the slide. I made the quarterly SE report all about what it meant for the sales team in an easy-to-read fashion.

Before you prepare your reporting, review and validate your numbers. Your raw data won't be complete. Very often, I would need to fill in a couple of places where SEs forgot to report activity. Or a record would have the wrong date or be associated with the wrong customer. It's important to get your CRM system updated appropriately, so keep a note of the adjustments you make so you can ask your SEs to make the necessary changes in the system – or do it yourself if you can. That said, don't kill yourself fixing everything. As stated before, good is always good enough. Data that is 70% complete is useful for the types of decisions you need to make.

Once you've done your data review, look for outliers. You want to identify anything that is a major change from what's usual so you can provide an explanation. *Very often, the explanation is some correction you needed to make in the data that you missed.* When it's not, it's usually then attributed to a large deal that skews the numbers or a change in the people on the team (losing or gaining). Once you rule these out, what you have is a result of a change in the way you delivered the service. In these situations, you want to make sure you dig deep to understand what changed and why. For outliers of this nature, investigate the associated deals and deal activity. Determine an explanation and indicate whether this is something systemic to be corrected or a one-time occurrence that won't occur again. This is the stuff in which the sales team will be interested!

Review

Before you review it with anyone else, review the data and analysis with your team. Get their perspective and make sure to include it. This is a great way to show them how the data your collecting is used. It helps them understand what they can contribute to improving performance and closing more deals. You'll get more direct insight from the people doing the job. It will also lead to better data input. Your SE team will be invested in the use of data and want to make sure it accurately reflects what's going on in the field.

Now distribute this to your sales partners, the consumers of the SE services. Share it with them whether they ask for it or not. You may also get the opportunity to present this information at the Sales QBR. If you're not on the agenda for that meeting, you should ask to be. If not, the schedule a separate time to review with the relevant sales leadership. Your input and analysis are important to improving the overall sales process. If you're not part of the discussion, sales leadership is missing an important and necessary perspective.

Adjust

The end goal of all of this is to be able to adjust what and how you deliver to find and close more deals. The work of defining, monitoring, evaluating, presenting, and reviewing is to make sure that what you're doing is optimal. If it is, then you determine what you need to keep going. If it isn't, you use the data and input and work with your SE and Sales team to figure out what to change.

The danger here when you determine you need to improve is to over adjust. Only in rare occasions would you ever need to completely rework the way your team delivers something. You may need to add a demo use case or two. Or adjust the way you demonstrate a capability. You'll have new features to incorporate into your demo, or a competitor's new feature to address. Usually, smaller adjustments give you improved results. And if you throw away something and start over, there is no real way to know if what you try next will help.

Let me provide a detailed story from my past. When I first joined a fast growth startup, there were 3 SEs on the team. Doing a POC – taking data from the prospect and configuring it into the solution – was a key part of every sales cycle. The solution helped build cost models; something customers normally did using Excel. It was a big shift for most, and they needed to work with the platform before they would be convinced. The sales teams would conduct the POC over the course of multiple months. They didn't push prospects but would prompt them from time to time.

Prospects would put various levels of effort into the POC. After some investigating, I learned that these efforts led to a closed deal only half the time. It put the deal on hold and kept the sales team from interacting with the prospect, as they still had day jobs and wouldn't commit focused time to the evaluation. The prospect would fit it in when they could. It was up to the sales team to put all the energy it could into progressing the deal.

This was the first SE service I decided to change. While many wanted to avoid a POC, I believed that doing the activity was the best way to show a prospect how the platform worked. I also believed it could be completed in a much shorter period and with a higher degree of interaction. We were able to convince one of our prospects to provide us with two hours. In that time, we walked them through the basics of how to build a cost model, using their data. The results were incredibly positive. With our help, it was much easier for the prospect to see value vs. attempting to let them use the product on their own. And we could focus on what would be valuable to them, not just on capability.

We re-branded the POC service to be a POV – Proof of Value. We put a structure to it, asking prospects to give us dedicated time. Our give to them was a shorter and more valuable process. We even suggested that we wouldn't allow prospects to do the evaluation themselves. At the same time, we began monitoring POV success rate (number of times doing a POV led to a closed deal) and POV duration (number of days from receiving data to presenting results). With this new way of delivering, the success rate increased to over 70% in the next quarter. And in looking at all the POVs we delivered, *those that led to a closed deal had the shortest duration*. Those that led to a lost deal – where the prospect decided not to select us – took longer. And those POVs that led to no decision - meaning the prospect stopped communicating – took longer still.

The combination of this change and the above data were able to convince the sales team that POVs done the way we recommended were better than simply allowing the prospects to do what they wanted. And not engaging in a POV until the prospect agreed to collaborate with us was also essential. We convinced them that using a POV to keep the deal going really didn't work. Average POV duration soon dropped to 30 days and the success rate increased to over 80%.

Using this internal service provider mindset not only gave me a way to better understand how to improve the SE team's performance, but it also provided a way to talk about what we did and why to others. Combining data with the real-world experience was the combination that helped us understand what needed to change and how best to adjust it.

Make It Operational

As you use the service delivery framework over time, you'll discover the set of metrics you'll want to monitor and evaluate consistently. What you choose will depend on the nature of the sales cycle, how technical the sell is, deal size, who you sell to, and what activities the SE team needs to perform to achieve the technical win. As the SE Leader, you should assemble these core metrics into one place and review them no more than monthly. Looking at smaller time increments isn't useful unless you're dealing with sales cycles that happen in less than a month.

Here's a list of metrics that I've used effectively in the past:

Metric	Calculation	Use
POV Success Rate	Percent of time that a POC or POV lead to a closed deal.	I used this to determine if POCs, the biggest effort and biggest risk for the SE team, were being conducted in the right way.
POV Duration	Average number of days from when a POV started until it was completed. It's important to standardize the events that occur to indicate start and finish, otherwise this data was useless.	This helped determine the level of effort – the commitment needed from the SE team – to get a POV done. It also helped me understand SE team capacity and when I might need more help.

Metric	Calculation	Use
Avg time from POV Close to Closed Deal	Average number of days between the day a POV is completed and the day the customer provides their decision to buy or not.	The impact of a POV drops off dramatically after 3-4 weeks unless the sales team can continue to find ways to present results to the prospect. And POVs should be s closing activities. My target was to have a deal close within 30 days of completing the POV.
First Demo to Active Opportunity	This is the percentage of time that doing a demo leads to an active sales cycle.	One of the common complaints of SEs is being asked to demo when it's not appropriate. There is no way to know if that's happening without measuring this. And just because your percentage here is low doesn't mean your team is providing a demo at the wrong time. It could be they aren't providing the right demo. This will point you to that either way.
Technical Win Rate	The number of times the SE team achieves the Technical Win in a deal.	This is difficult to track as achieving the Technical Win is subjective. Sometimes the prospect clearly indicates it, sometimes they don't. It's also possible to achieve the Technical Win without winning the deal. Make sure the AE on the deal agrees that you achieved a Technical Win, or this metric will have no credibility.
Hire to First Demo	The average number of days between an SE being hired and them delivering their first demo independently.	A bit of a curveball. Onboarding, especially when you're in growth mode, is damn important, especially for SEs. No SE likes to feel like they can't be used. Depending on what you sell, this number should be 30 days or less if possible.

Converting Metrics to KPIs

The above metrics by themselves help you establish a baseline. If you haven't consistently been collecting metrics, you shouldn't attempt to interpret anything from them initially. Instead, look to make connections between metric values and what you see happening in the field. Once you believe you have some basic connections, you can now set targets and work to change SE behavior to achieve those targets. For me, this was how I evolved from using metrics to using time bound KPIs. KPIs become the elements you use to help you make decisions on what activities to adjust and how to adjust them.

Putting it All Together.

Operating the service delivery process on a regular basis becomes the way you manage the SE team as if it's a business. Every quarter you should engage with your team and the AEs and analyze the previous quarters data. Decide on the actions you want to take to make improvements and get agreement on how best to take those actions. Then begin the process again.

Develop your five slides – your consistent quarterly report. I would suggest it have the following elements:

- Recap of the past quarter: Narrative of how successful the quarter was and insights of what you understand from the KPIs. This should include the KPIs themselves.
- A summary of the deal activity with analysis of why you won, why you lost, and what the SE team's part was in all of that.
- A narrative on the state of the team itself – for example, how many hired, how the talent progressed, and how morale is.
- What elements of the company, the business, or the market changed in the quarter that effect how the SE Team works

and the services it provides, with the specific impact of each item.

- What your plan is for the next quarter to address what you've outlined above.

What you'll find is that very quickly this quarterly report morphs from something you do as a historical exercise to something you look at regularly during the quarter to something that helps guide your decision making and how you manage the team.

Conclusion

Constantly striving to be better and to win is part of every SEs nature. It takes more than intuition and gut feel to understand how to do that. The only way to know whether your SE team is doing the right things and doing them well is to measure, consistently, over time. Then connect those measurements to the activity and results you see in the field. Armed with this, you can collaborate with your team and the rest of the business to suggest improvements to services and track the impact of those suggestions. You can have real business level discussions about the value the SE team provides and elevate its role to being strategic.

5: Augment

Hiring is damn important. And the most important if you're working in a small but fast-growing company. I've heard people managers talk about how hiring gets in the way of their "day job." I can only shake my head when I hear this and wonder what they think their day job really is.

Most of the hiring I've witnessed is done ad hoc. Most of the HR support came in the form of restrictions on recruiting, limiting comp plans, and insisting on updating the recruiting system to make sure that HR had visibility into everything that was happening. Hiring managers would do a phone screen then grab a few other people with whom the candidate could speak. In some cases, those who were asked to talk to the candidate in turn asked the hiring manager if there were specific things they should investigate. The hiring manager would say something like "I'm just looking for your impression of her." Then the group of people who spoke to the candidate would get together and talk about those impressions and thoughts. Each interviewer used their own gut feel. They focused on the things they thought were potentially important. There wasn't much of a standard set of interview criteria or certainly any kind of measurement. Most of the conversations were less than an hour, so there was a tremendous reliance on those first impressions. If everyone had positive feelings, the candidate would get an offer.

In addition to that, most candidates were initially selected based on an extremely limited profile. Hiring managers would identify their best people and say: “I need to get more of those. If only there were cloning machines...” Executives and HR would agree: “Yes! Give me a whole team of those people.” The internal recruiter would scour LinkedIn for people with the same title who had worked at the same companies and had the same level of experience. And those people are quite difficult to find. They form a limited candidate pool that is in demand, as your competitors are doing the same thing. And those people know they have the upper hand. They’re entertaining many suitors and multiple offers and asking for outrageous compensation. And getting it. And, when hired, usually not providing the value and output for which they’re overpaid. The Law of Diminishing Returns flattened the value curve on that type of hiring quickly and significantly.

Instead of the clone, you settled for whoever remained. Someone that seemed good enough. You knew in your heart that this person would never be an A player. But you needed to get roles filled. You hired, and then rolled up your sleeves preparing to put a lot of investment in helping that person get up to speed. Or being ready to carry a lot of the load yourself.

This paints a very bleak picture on the quality of hiring in tech. And perhaps it is a tad exaggerated for effect. After all, there are some examples of fast growth tech startups that followed this path, grew fast, did an IPO, and made millions – or even billions. And if this is your path – grow fast, IPO quickly, and then not care – you can skip this chapter. In fact, go quickly and get as many clones as you can before the other startups get them!

If, instead, you are looking to maximize the value of the investment you make in hiring, keep going. It is possible to hire outside of the limited profile represented by your best SEs. In fact*, it is actually BETTER for you and the team to do so*. Rather than simply adding to your team, you can *Augment* it.

To Augment means *to make something greater by adding to it.* When you hire, don't just think about adding capacity or making sure you have enough SEs to supply demos for sales. Instead, *use a comprehensive talent profile and measure cognitive diversity to increase the SE team's ability to innovate, change, and perform*. What follows is my guidance on how to do that.

The A Player Principle

Here is the first of what may be several controversial statements. I believe that you can have a team made up entirely of A players or those with the potential to be A Players. The notion that you must settle for a mix of overall capabilities – that you'll always have B and C players on your team – is wrong.

And wouldn't it be amazing to have a team of all A Players? If you're willing to entertain the idea, let me explain.

First, let's put some clear definition to what an A Player is. An A Player is *someone who autonomously and consistently delivers the right outcomes at the highest levels of quality*. They aren't perfect, but they are consistent and dependable. These are the SEs that you assign to a deal with complete confidence, knowing you most likely won't have to lift a finger to help them. The sales team comfortably relies on them. They don't need your constant attention and direction. They appreciate any coaching you give because A Players always seek to improve. Related, the A Player Potential is someone who, with the right coaching and enablement from you, will operate as an A Player. They have the right combination of innate ability, personality traits, capacity to learn, and motivation. With your help, they too will autonomously and consistently deliver the right outcomes at the highest level of quality.

I define a B or C player as someone who will not ever be able to deliver the right outcomes autonomously and consistently at the highest levels of quality. The amount of coaching and enablement required is too great. You'll need to provide too much oversight. You won't be able to use those SEs for all opportunities, just the easiest and least risky. You'll need to be careful about which AE you pair them with. And even then, you'll still worry about the outcome. I don't look at these labels (A, B, C) as levels an SE progresses through. The person either had the potential or doesn't. If they don't, there is a role somewhere in the world for which they would have the potential. And that's where they need to be.

The first objection to this notion may be that it's impossible to scale such a team. There simply aren't enough A Players or Potentials in the world. I know many people – especially sales leaders – think that great SEs are more like mythical creatures. They are rare or don't exist at all. I don't subscribe to that notion. There are plenty of amazing SEs and potential SEs in the market. You just need to change your way of thinking and your notion of the ideal candidate. Stop looking for clones. Don't think that the only candidates you should consider are those that already have sales engineer experience in the same area of tech. That's not the case. Erase the whiteboard in your head that has that long and restrictive list, that ridiculously small and limiting profile into which a good candidate must fit. It's time to start considering a much broader range of people using a different filter.

The next objection may be that this will simply take too long. You'll need to kiss lots of frogs. Yes, to be successful following this principle will require a greater investment in time than you are making now. You'll need consider a greater number of candidates. You'll need to have more and longer conversations. As you rethink the profile of the candidates to seek, there will be a lot of learning. You'll need to do a lot of fine tuning. You'll need to be creative in who you consider and then spend more time with them to determine if they will be good. *The payoff will be that you won't need as many people on your team to provide the same or greater level of service.*

You may be getting pressure from HR or your management, concerned that if you don't fill the open positions, you will lose them. It's a valid concern. There are optics. Internally, some will wonder if you are being too fussy or too afraid to make a bad choice. Externally, people will wonder why a job is open for so long. Is the company too choosy? Is it so bad that people interview and then aren't interested in pursuing it? The real question is not whether you'll fill the position. The question is whether it is better to have someone who isn't going to be great vs having no one at all. I would contend with you that, if you have a team of A Players, it's better for you to run lean than carry the weight of someone who doesn't meet that standard. It ends up creating more work for you, and it's a morale dampener for the rest of the team.

If you believe this is simply too complicated and too much work, then I would suggest that you are abdicating your second greatest responsibility as an SE manager. *And the first is not close business.* And neither is the second. The SE Manager's first job is to do everything they can to ensure the team they have is the best they can be. The second is to find more great SEs to be part of that team.

Don't simply trust me. This isn't a new notion. My inspiration comes from the book *Topgrading* by Bradford Smart. It was his book that inspired me to find out for myself if this is true. The book is THICK, but the first few chapters and the last were enough to make me think about hiring and interviewing in a completely different way. I was willing to then put the work in to prove it out. And it was well worth it, as most hard work is.

So, throw away the idea that you need to grab whatever SE candidate you can to fill your open positions quickly. Dispense with the idea that you will be stuck with a blend of A, B, and C players, and that you should just play to the average. You don't have to, and you should not.

Defining the A Player

To find and hire your A Players, you need to dispense with the typical job description that outlines the experience and skills you expect a candidate to have. That is not a broad enough definition. It describes the job, but it doesn't describe the best candidates. As I hope you'll come to believe, there are many potential candidate profiles that will be able to successfully do that job. Step back and think about a broader set of elements that a candidate needs to have to be a successful SE. Let me suggest these four categories:

Knowledge

This is what an SE needs to know and to what depth they need to know it to be successful in their role. It includes knowledge about your solution, the industry it serves, and the people that use and benefit from the solution. As you consider these elements, think about how easy it is to acquire this requisite knowledge. There are many things you can understand from books or courses. There are some things to which you just need experience to know it. The things to which you need experience don't belong in this category – so drop those down to Experience (we'll get there). Consider this category to be knowledge that the candidate already has or that they can acquire through some learning channel.

I think about that knowledge in several areas: Industry, product, personas and use cases. Industry is the general understanding of the business which your solution operates. It's an understanding of how that business works and what the people in that business do.

Product is the knowledge not only of the product you sell but of the other products in the ecosystem that do the same or related things. Personas are the roles of the people that will use or benefit from your solution. And use cases are the business activities your solution supports.

For all categories, list all the different topics associated to the business and technology related to your solution. Think about the depth of knowledge an A Player SE should have. As I considered these things, I defined four levels of depth:

- **No Knowledge**: Knew nothing about the topic other than terms or its existence.
- **Basic Understanding**: Understood terms and could speak at a high level about it.
- **Working Knowledge**: Knows not only terms but the basics of the business processes and who operates them, as well as the tools they use. Has a basic understanding of the challenges people operating these processes face.
- **In Depth**: Can describe in detail the business processes themselves and the tools used in those processes. Can talk in terms of best practices and real-world examples.

This is a subjective exercise. There is no one way to define these levels. It will depend on the industry in which you work, and the technology used in that industry. The most important thing to do is make this useful for your hiring. Don't initially over engineer it. Be willing to adjust as you use it and learn more.

If I think about the business of accounting and accounting software, I might suggest a candidate with *No Knowledge* would only know that accounting was a financial practice and no more. A candidate with *Basic Understanding* would know that accounting is a practice to manage the finances of a business and consisted of creating and updating a general ledger, balance sheet, and various reporting. Someone with *Working Knowledge* would know there was a quarterly cadence to accounting practices. They would understand the different between operating expense and capital expenditure. They would know what depreciation was, as it related to capital assets. They would also know that accountants used Excel, and that ERP systems like SAP or Oracle supported accounting functions. A candidate with *In-Depth* knowledge would know that different companies favor operating expense over capital spend and why. They would understand the techniques that internal accountants used to build the cost center structure to make a company's financial health and reporting seem as favorable as possible.

Skills

This is what an SE needs to be able to do, and to what degree of proficiency. Before you sit down with a blank screen and start typing that list, if you've followed Advance, you already have some of what you need. Under Evaluate, I introduced you to the rubric framework to define what good delivery of your SE services looks like. From these rubrics, you can easily extract the skills a candidate needs to be an A Player. Simply look at the Exceptional column for each of the components of the service. Those are the capabilities and behaviors exhibited by an A Player. There will most likely be duplicates across the various SE services, so some aggregation will give you a consolidated list.

If you refer to *Figure 3: Portion of a Demo Rubic*, you'll remember that it highlights the right way to setup the demonstration as well as presentation style cues. Reviewing this, you might add the following list of skills to the profile of an A Player SE:

- When presenting, the SE varies tone of voice and pace to enhance clarity and emphasize important points.
- SE understands the concept of a disruptive truth and knows how and when to employ it during presentations and demonstrations.

- SE can associate the proprietary benefits of the solution to an individual prospect's needs and articulate how that benefit will fill that need using the prospect's language.

You need to make the skills specific enough that the SE is clear on the expectations but not so specific that you have too many to manage. The rubrics will form a significant part of how you measure proficiency in these skills, but you may need to determine others.

As with knowledge, the level of proficiency required will determine how much investment you need to put into a candidate that doesn't have the skill. Consider some of these skills as potential must-haves, meaning the candidate should already have that skill. For the others, create a plan to get a candidate that doesn't have the skill onboarded as soon as possible.

Experience

This outlines the situations and people with whom you would like a candidate to have worked. It's an interesting topic when it comes to becoming a sales engineer. I do not believe that someone can step into a customer-facing sales engineer position straight out of academia. I also think the same applies to anyone who takes an SE training course but has no industry or in-role experience. The business-to-business (B2B) sales process is something to which you need to be exposed before you can operate successfully in it. There may be some business-to-consumer (B2C) or smaller transaction B2B sales in which an SE without exposure may be successful with training only. Otherwise, there are experiences the candidate should have before you put them into the role.

As you think about hiring, you need to decide what experiences a candidate needs to have coming in and what they can reasonably acquire in the job. You may, for example, hire an SE who understands the role but has no exposure to the business you support. For the first six months, you have them operate in an apprentice capacity. They shadow demo meetings, build custom demos, work on POCs, and do as much “behind the scenes” activity as they can to be exposed to your business. Once they’ve had a certain amount of exposure, they will be confident to effectively communicate and demonstrate the value of your solutions to your target audience.

Traits

This is what makes up an SE’s personality and natural aptitudes. Think of these for the most part as intangibles, personality characteristics, behaviors, and aptitudes the SE has because of who they are. These are things like self-confidence, responsibility, work ethic, and problem-solving ability.

Putting it Together

For each of these elements – the KSET –define what an A player SE would have and to what degree. Determine which of these a candidate must bring with them vs. what they can learn on the job. The KSET will be unique to your organization and most likely to the role if you specialize within the SE team.

This is a lot to consider – but great hiring is worth the effort. Imagine how much easier your day-to-day job is if all the SEs you manage operate autonomously and consistently deliver high quality work and outcomes. Imagine also if, when you sat down to interview someone, you knew exactly what you wanted to ask and how to direct the conversation. When you were done, you not only felt like you knew that person well enough to decide about them, but you could also easily compare them to the other candidates with whom you spoke because your conversations were consistently about the same things.

In fact, take the time to imagine that now. Hopefully, that gets you excited enough to dive into this immediately, even if you’re in the middle of hiring. The only thing between you and the team of A players is this effort.

Let me relay a story from my past that really helped to significantly shape my thinking. During my time at a startup, I built a team of what I called Technical Solutions Engineers. This team was not customer facing but instead was intended to support all the technical validation activity by creating demonstrations and doing configuration work for Proof of Value exercises. I intended to bring on people with no SE experience and develop them into customer-facing Solution Consultants.

I was hiring for this team and was asked to consider the friend of our internal recruiter. Her friend had no experience in B2B sales or in configuring software. What she did have was experience in finance and in using Excel to do financial analysis and reporting. Given that was part of the solution, there was at least some possibility that she could fit in the role. Had she blindly submitted a resume, I probably would not have considered her. I was convinced I needed someone with more technical and B2B experience.

To my surprise, she smashed the interview. What I discovered was someone who had a diverse background, a capacity to learn quickly, an amazing work ethic, and an extremely positive attitude. I started the interview thinking I would do the polite thing because she was a referral, but that there would really be no way I would consider her. When the interview ended, she had sold me on her ability to be an A Player in the role. I hired her. The knowledge of the industry and our product that she didn't have, she was able to learn. She acquired the skills to configure the software to support our selling efforts. She had no background or experience in sales, but through the experience of working on different sales cycles came to be respected as someone who knew how to best position the product in a technical evaluation.

In the time she was at the company, she then earned a promotion to manage the Technical Solutions Engineer team. She established a great reputation among the company's leadership. She was then approached by the head of engineering to manage one of the development teams. She literally went from being a financial analyst to being a software engineering manager in a few short years. I was willing to be open-minded, and as a result, learned a valuable lesson about what an A Player could look like.

I do not think she was an outlier or a unicorn. When I think about the A Player sales engineers I know, they have diverse educational backgrounds and work experience. They don't all fit the limited mold of technical university degrees and technical backgrounds. What they had was a great foundation of the right knowledge, skills, experience, and traits with the ability, attitude, and work ethic to acquire the rest of what they needed. They became sales engineers that delivered high quality work autonomously and consistently.

Building and Using the KSET Profile

Let me share another example from that same company to help you understand how to pull it all together. The solution provided a platform to help IT organizations understand how much things like their applications cost. It required combining traditional accounting data with technical IT data. An A Player SE then needed to understand business accounting AND the complicated world of the IT environment: servers, network, applications, storage, cloud. Taken separately, these are quite different fields of knowledge. It was rare to find someone with even Basic Knowledge of both. The trick was determining which knowledge was more difficult to teach. What I learned through a bit of trial and error was that an SE candidate with Basic Knowledge of accounting had the potential to be an A Player. They didn't need to be a CPA. The IT knowledge was much more complicated, more important to selling the solution, and much more difficult to teach. When I hired candidates that had experience with accounting software but no technical knowledge, the learning gap was too big to fill. The right training material wasn't readily available. It took a long time to get those new hires up to speed. They would get frustrated and decide the role wasn't right for them. The accounting knowledge was much easier to teach an SE with knowledge of IT vs. the other way around. The candidate requirements I created preferred those with Working Knowledge or better of IT.

From a skills perspective, understanding how to do defensible data analysis was also important. It wasn't enough to build a cost model. An A Player SE needed to be able to explain how to make it useful, and in the context of sometimes extremely limited data. They had to know where to make some assumptions and what assumptions were valid. There were additional skills that supported this data analysis, like being able to use Excel to do some initial assessment of the data, as well as creating HTML tags to be able to do formatting. In addition to the skills described in the Demo and POV Rubric, I added data analysis and explanation.

Experience was a natural follow on to skills. Think of experience in two parts: the experience of using the skill for a job (like data analysis), and the experience of being in a role where you are exposed to the knowledge and skills that are important. In this case, someone who had been a business analyst in IT, or even been an internal business liaison to the IT organization, may not have done any data analysis themselves, but they were exposed to such things and therefore had a level of comfort with them. Sometime, that level of comfort was all that was necessary vs. having been in role and done the actual work.

Traits really are the most critical of the four. The most useful Traits simply can't be taught. They are abilities that someone is born with. Some people's brains naturally understand languages well. Speaking many languages fluently isn't an impossible ask. Others struggle with their own language let alone attempting to learn another (my hand raised). But those same people may be better with numbers – doing arithmetic in their heads simply happens. My son at an early age could look at a map and simply remember it. We could get in the car, and he could provide turn-by-turn directions. His mother, on the other hand, didn't trust herself to know where she was going even after having been someplace several times.

This also extends beyond brain capabilities to personality. Most people who work in business have taken a personality assessment, like Myers-Briggs, Color Insights, or Clarity 4D. These help you understand your preferences and how you should best interact with others and be interacted with. This is also an important aspect of Traits. I encourage you to investigate the science behind this and the various frameworks that are available. Applying them is highly beneficial in helping you understand what traits an A Player should have AND how they can best be hired and managed.

Once you've identified the KSETs and decided the level of understanding or ability is necessary for each, you've got an A Player Profile.

Here are some final words of advice. You will most likely over engineer your first attempt. You think about ALL the potentials and are worried about missing something. I would suggest that once you've made your first pass, force yourself to remove at least 20% of the KSETs in each category.

Once you've done that, look at what's left and determine which of these things a candidate needs to bring with them and which you can help them acquire after hire. Your ideal candidate has all of it, but this exercise is about widening the net. So be stingy with what you consider the must-haves. A Player Potential means that this person CAN have all the KSETs you define to the degree you want them, but not at the time of hire.

Now that you know what you're looking for, build an interview guide to evaluate for it. For each piece of Knowledge, Skill, Experiences, and Traits, fashion a list of questions that help you determine what the candidate has and to what degree. Shape questions so that you can tease out specific examples and in-depth stories, not just general responses. You'll find this guide will help you get to know a candidate to a degree that you'll feel comfortable choosing them over the remaining candidates. You'll be able to extend an offer with more confidence than you have before about what you'll be getting when that person starts.

The Most Important Consideration

There is one final element to consider as you think about your A Player profile – as if there hasn't been enough discussed. This one calls for its own section, despite it not being a long one. It has to do with the most important relationship in technical sales.

Understand that no SE will be an A Player in your organization if they don't fit with their respective AE team. The AEs will most likely tell you that if you're happy with the candidate, they will be. I'm sure their intention is good. It's just not practical. It doesn't make sense to hire a meticulous SE if your sales reps like to work fast and loose. Or the opposite – if you have a very sales-oriented SE and you try to pair them with sales reps who are methodical and want the SE to be part of every step in the sales cycle. Despite everyone's best intentions, this won't lead to a team of A Players.

How the SE will fit with the AE team will ultimately make or break their success. Once you have found a potential A Player, make sure they can gel with the AE's. Their success and yours depends on it.

The Process to Find Them

There are lots of ways to go about finding and hiring the A Players. What's important is that you define your process and inform everyone who will be involved (especially your HR business partner). What I outline here is the process I followed which worked well in case you find it beneficial.

First, let me offer some guiding principles. They are:

- It's worse to hire a bad fit than miss hiring a good one. Which is not to say that missing a good hire is ok. It's not. It just means that taking a chance on someone you're not completely sure of isn't worth it.
- Any doubt from anyone in the process is a good reason to say no. Get comfortable with saying no and sticking to the profile you create. The good news is that your new profile opens your search to many more candidates. The bad news is that means you'll need to go through more candidates to get to the A Players. Have the patience to do that.
- For every candidate to whom you say no, you're one candidate closer to your A Player. It's a bit cliché and cheesy, but it's true. And it helps you feel better about the No's.

Here is the process itself:

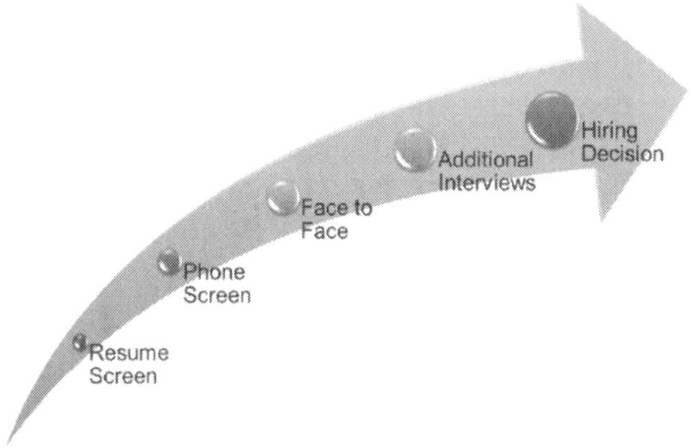

Figure 4: The Hiring Process

This is very straightforward. That said, it still contains more due diligence than most of the hiring in which I've been involved. The key is making sure everyone involved is aware of the process and your expectations. Let me review what I believe to be important in each step.

Resume Screen

This is where being different starts. It's not something you can delegate to an internal recruiter with no experience with SEs. And at first, you'll want to do this yourself. You need to do some exploring. There is nothing wrong with starting with candidates with SE experience that sell related solutions, or solutions that might have the same capabilities or solve similar problems. As you expand your search, look for people that work in industry (the K and E from the KSET). Then perhaps in related industries. One of my best sources of non-traditional candidates was the larger, global consulting firms. You can find people with customer facing experience and knowledge of the industry. If a candidate then has the right traits, the rest can be taught.

Phone Screen

Before you invest a serious amount of time with someone, you should get past the first impression. You should decide whether:

- You have the desire to spend more time with them
- You have the confidence to introduce them to the other people involved in the process

I used to be one of those hiring managers that spoke with the candidate for the full hour, even if in the first 5-10 minutes I knew I wasn't going to move them through the process. I know many people feel that ending the interview early may be rude or hurtful. I've come to believe that keeping an interview going when you already know the outcome is ruder. While ending early may be surprising, it's better to break what may be disappointing news as soon as possible. It's better for both of you to reclaim the time. Interviewing can be exhausting work. You should only put as much time into a candidate as is necessary to decide whether they should continue. And one bit of doubt for me was enough to stop. I also learned to stop assuming that the candidate was interested in working for me. I'm quite sure there were many candidates who had decided that in the first 5 minutes but were too polite to say anything.

This meeting should be 30 minutes. It's first a likability test. Given the proliferation of video technology, it should be done virtually face to face. You should be prepared with a couple of questions based on your KSET profile that you know are deal breakers. Focus on Traits. You should also ask the candidate what their expectations are for the role and from the organization. That should be enough to tell you whether you have a viable candidate or not.

Face to Face

The name is a throwback to a time when the first conversation was on the phone with the hopes of getting to an actual in person meeting – before you could very easily do a virtual meeting that included video. Times are now hugely different, but I didn't have a better name for this step. I guess I could have called it The Big Meeting or The Test or something more ominous and grandiose.

I suggest you plan 3 hours for this meeting. This is also where I typically get the most protest. If you've built the interview guide as I've suggested above, it will take some time to cover it all. You also need to give the candidate ample time to get to know you and ask questions.

Deciding about how you're going to spend 8+ hours of your day, 5 days a week, is a huge decision. Massive. Many people take it too lightly. Any candidate that doesn't want to really get to know who will be telling them what to do with that time probably isn't worth the interview. Deciding on someone who will have a large bearing on whether you are successful in your role or not is also a massive decision. Any hiring manager who doesn't want to spend enough time to determine if that candidate will bring them success or failure should probably find something else to do.

I'm not suggesting you grill the candidate for 3 straight hours. Take breaks. Switch in the middle of the meeting and allow the candidate to ask questions before you go back to asking more. Make it as conversational and comfortable as possible. Encourage the candidate to tell stories. Press for more detail where you can. You will hear things that are familiar, but don't assume what their saying aligns to what you're thinking. Ask the same question in different ways throughout the interview to see if you get the same answer. Spending this kind of time allows you to get past the candidate's "job interview answers" and get to really knowing the person.

Additional Interviews

At this point you should be ready to hire the candidate. But they have probably not encountered the other people with whom they'll have to work. I suggest you have your SE candidate speak with

- 1-2 more SEs from the team, maybe even as a group interview
- The first line sales manager from the sales team they would support
- At least 1 AE
- Your HR business partner
- Potentially someone from product marketing and customer success.

The ideal way and best use of time would be to line up these meetings on the same day or consecutive days. An hour with your existing SE and 30 minutes with everyone else should be enough.

This is as much about the candidate deciding if they can collaborate with these people as it is them making the same decision about the candidate. Make sure the candidate understands this and encourage them to ask probing questions.

Hiring Decision

In the end, this is down to you. But I never hired a candidate where anyone of the other people in the process expressed any doubt. I suggest you meet with everyone together after they've all spoken with him. That way you can corroborate impressions to determine if you missed anything.

Then take a deep breath and make sure this is the person you want to bring into your team and bet your business on. If it is – well done. If not, don't make the offer. And well done. You've dropped someone from the list and can go find the right one.

Take the time to do this right. You may get resistance from candidates who are concerned about how much time they'll need to take away from their current job. You will hear concerns from HR or sales leadership about them not having the time to put into this or it not being their "day job." Resist the desire to give in to the easy route. And at the same time, continuously tune the process to optimize it. Make the process work for you. Your business depends on it.

Diversity May Not Be What You Think

Hiring can't be discussed without also mentioning the importance of diversity. My own views on diversity have changed significantly over the course of my career.

Early on, I had the opportunity to be involved in college recruiting for my company. It was a comprehensive program, and my employer took this very seriously. There was an on-campus component, where recruiters from our HR visited and identified potential candidates. To make the process as efficient as possible, we then flew all the potentials to our offices (which were spread out over an entire city) and gave them a day where we toured facilities and met with various managers and executives. The following day, they would spend the morning in 5 interviews a piece, then fly back to school. The interviewers would then gather to assess and rank the candidates and identify which open positions they best fit. At one point toward the end of one of the meetings, I was told one of the senior VPs looked at the list of the top candidates and told the group that there wasn't enough diversity. What he meant was that all the top candidates were white males, and they needed to swap out some white males for non-white male candidates.

I'll admit it angered me. I did not want to deny anyone an opportunity for a job. But in my naïve view, why couldn't the best candidate get that job regardless of skin color, gender, or heritage? I didn't realize how deeply ingrained the wrong thinking was. So much so, that the current attempt to fix it was completely misguided. The system they were using was designed to account for diversity, *not value it.* That system put the most emphasis on technical knowledge and skill. It gave a nod to what we would call soft skills. But it didn't bother to consider a whole wealth of other characteristics. This system led to a team of clones. If things don't change, the clones perform well. But everything changes, and a team of people who all act and think the same doesn't adapt well to change or shift quickly to take advantage of new ideas.

Real diversity is so much more than skin color or gender. It goes well beyond the limited perspective so many have been fighting about and what government legislation dictates. Considering diversity in hiring isn't just about giving everyone a fair chance. If you put that aside and focus on the true value of diversity, you'll see everyone does get a chance after all. The true value of diversity is in the combining of different perspectives, ways of thinking, and approaches to problem-solving that as a result bring about real innovation and new solutions. You could hire a team of A players that all fit the same profile. They would all have sales engineer experience from companies in the same space that bit similar or related products. They would all have sold to the same personas. They would all have remarkably similar skill sets. Their demos would probably all look and sound about the same. You might even congratulate yourself on a job well done. And for a time, you may find your team successful. If you're in a stable tech sector where there isn't a ton of innovation, this may be exactly the team you need.

But more than likely, things will change – whether it's the technology or the business climate. And when that change happens, you'll need to change to adjust and take advantage of new opportunities. You'll find that will be difficult to do with your team of clones. They, unfortunately, only have a limited perspective, based on the experience and education they have. Their approach to addressing the change will be similar. If it's effective, great. If it's not, you're stuck. And even putting aside having to address some external factor. Good teams – great teams – are always looking for new and better ways of doing things. A team comprised of people with similar experience, education, and background will be very limited in conceiving new and better ways.

What you need to consider is building real diversity into your candidate search and evaluation process. Use your KSET profile to determine not only how to get out of pursuing the same candidate profile but to be purposeful in doing it. Where you bring in diversity is in considering the path that your candidates took to acquire their knowledge and skills. In addition, look outside of the KSET at the individual. University degrees, technical certifications, and past roles are only a part of the person, and perhaps not a majority part. Include in your consideration the things they like to do, experiences they seek outside of their wage earning. Looking at the whole person will give you a sense for all the tools and energy they would bring to your team to help generate innovation.

Let me give you an example. Consider the two groups of people:

Figure 5: Two Groups of Candidates

Even without seeing their color, you can see that Group A seems mostly homogenous while Group B appears more diverse. Now consider the same two groups of people after adding some personal and professional information about them.

Figure 6: Two Groups of Candidates with Profiles

If we take everything we know about these individuals into account, it's fair to say Group A may in fact be a bit more diverse than Group B, or at the very least there is a similar level of diversity along different factors.

To achieve a team that provides greater variability in their thinking and problem solving, I would probably want Group A. They come from different countries – so have a diverse cultural background. They have more variability in their level of experience, how they were educated, and in their current home life. There is amazing value in pulling a team like this together and learning how to harness its diversity to power improvement and innovation. I will leave it to you to research, but there is plenty of evidence that teams with this type of diversity drive greater innovation, have higher employee engagement, and better employee performance.

When it comes to selling, SEs can use all the innovation they can get. To successfully sell, a solution needs to stand out. Sales teams are constantly looking for ways to be unique and noticeable, to distinguish themselves from their competition and be remembered by their prospects. Your SE team can be a source of innovation to help create those distinctions and be the standout solution.

Ensuring you consider diversity of background, experiences, personalities, origin, and education can help you create a team that not only performs well now but knows how to improve and can be agile and innovative in adjusting to changes in business and technology.

Conclusion

Hiring to build your team is the second most important thing you do as a people manager next to taking care of the team you have. It's an activity that deserves the appropriate amount of time to ensure you bring on the best people you can. You should strive to build a team that only consists of A players or those that have the potential to be A players. To do that means defining what an A player really looks like. It means not cloning your best SE, but really understanding what knowledge, skills, experience, and traits best define the A player, and then going and acquiring that. At the same time, you can hire for innovation as well. By including diversity as a core part of your candidate search and assessment process, you can ensure a high performing team in the short term and a team that can improve and adapt to change through innovation and the combination of different perspectives – a truly Augmented team.

6: Advocate

It always bothered me how disconnected from my company I felt as a remote working SE. And I think to a degree it bothers most. Remember the SE Hierarchy of Needs. SEs want to be part of something bigger than themselves. They want to see the contribution they make. They like to have the opportunity to have a say in what goes in the product, or at least advocate on behalf of their customers. They like to be recognized on a broader stage for their expertise and accomplishments. This is hard to do when you spend most of your time in your bedroom on Zoom, or waiting to take a flight in an airport, or trying to kill time in a hotel room.

At the same time, those SEs who do make a connection with people at corporate always greatly benefit. While most SEs would build their own slides because they couldn't find anything they considered good, these SEs would get the latest from product marketing, or even something bespoke just for them. Their dev buddy would give them access to a future release or some screen shots, which they would whip out for that big customer to push a deal over the edge. You would see their face on webinar promotions or see them speaking at sales kick off. The AEs loved them, and the other SEs envied them. I always marveled at how they found the time to make those connections. I considered them workaholics – married to their jobs.

I also thought of them as being political, which I equated to being shallow and self-centered. This was my own jealousy, because of course while I didn't admit it, I wanted to be like them. They were well known. And they got stuff done. They were typically the ones helping to push the company forward. When I got to know them, I realized they weren't being political, or shallow, or self-centered. They behaved as they did, actively building relationships across various parts of the company, because they genuinely believed in what they were doing and enjoyed it. They really wanted to be part of it all and see it succeed. They were really into being SEs.

This behavior was typically based on the individual. It wasn't systemic or part of the organization. There were no corporate rules, mandates, team objectives that inspired or motivated this kind of collaboration. No manager coordinated this effort. It happened on its own. And it was not commonplace.

Imagine, though, if this wasn't the case. Imagine an SE organization mapped into the company it supports, having a constant flow of collaboration and ideas moving between them and marketing, products, customer success – every other part of the company. Imagine being able to tap into those departments as you sell, so the whole team had access to the best stuff. Imagine being able to have regular input into product direction and be the conduit for customers to have their voice heard. Imagine the whole company seeing the contribution the SE team makes, and the SE team feeling like they are an integral part of the company.

All of this is possible if you, the SE manager, learn to Advocate.

To Advocate means *to publicly recommend or support something or someone*. It's most visible in the political arena when influential politicians support candidates at election time. It's taken on a whole new meaning in the world of social media, as brands tap into Influencers to reach their millions of followers to promote their product. The principle is basically the same. A known quantity – someone with position or reputation – makes a connection or provides the platform for someone not as well known to be seen and heard, to participate. In this case, you are the person of position or reputation. You need to become the Influencer, so that you can connect your team to the rest of the company. When you're successful doing that, you meet the needs of your SEs and bring their goodness to the rest of the company.

The Grassroots Principle

With the proliferation of social media, it's easy to instantly connect to thousands, even millions, of people. And there are many who use this power of connection to influence those who connect with them. I had no idea how powerful this was until my son exposed me to how this works in the eSports industry. There are people who wield incredible influence in eSports – and they DON'T EVEN PLAY VIDEO GAMES. There is an influencer who has gathered his following because he provides videos of himself commenting on videos of others playing various games. He's entertaining. He has a few million followers across several platforms. If you play, it's your desire to have this person provide commentary on one of your gaming sessions. That way, you get recognized and gain a bigger following. This person is also paid by consumer brands to mention their products in his videos or even do short advertisement for them.

While social media and community platforms are starting to gain traction, getting influence and making connections in the corporate world still needs to be done the old-fashioned way – with one relationship at a time. And it's much more powerful to do it this way. The relationships you need to build involve more than just clicking a like button or reposting something. They lead to closed deals, new effective messaging the whole sales team can use, a wildly successful customer, or innovative new offerings from the company.

You will probably always have one SE on your team that does it on her own. She's extroverted, friendly, and execution focused. In her mind, it's up to her to get it done. And she does it whether she's supposed to or not, whether someone tells her to do it or not. Because she believes it's the right thing to do. And most of the time this is good for the team, and you can support and encourage it.

But I would also suggest that this is something you systematize and not leave to ad hoc activity. You will most likely find yourself in situations where your team doesn't have some of the collateral or tools they need. And despite your best efforts, they won't have the bandwidth or capability to provide those things for themselves. You'll need help from others. In addition, those others also need you. The SE team has a unique and valuable perspective on customers, what's happening in the market, and the perceived value of your products. The rest of the company can value greatly from this perspective.

But there is typically no mandate that says – "Hey, go ask the SE team about this!" Collaboration between organizations is not generally systemic or regular. Anyone who hired into a tech startup on a fast growth path has seen it. Everyone has their job and gets it done. They know there aren't resources to help, so they get used to doing everything on their own. As the company grows, that approach becomes ingrained. Instead of taking the time to step back and optimize across departments, these departments hire, grow, and operate on their own. And a company of siloed groups operating inefficiently is born. It takes deliberate effort to break this trend and start to think across departments.

Also, people don't always like to share. They may feel threatened. The thought of involving others or collaborating means sharing the credit or not getting any at all. They wonder then how they'll be able to advance. Or they worry they won't be able to hold on to their job because they won't be seen as contributing to anything. These patterns are natural ways in which the automatic side of the human brain works. We need to be aware and act deliberately to change them.

That's where the **Grassroots Principle** comes in. I use a little poetic license with the term, but I think the spirit of the meaning will be clear. For the SE team to get value from the other parts of the company, and for them to value the SEs, it takes a grassroots effort. I have most often heard this term applied to legal or political efforts for change, when that effort begins with ordinary citizens who reach out, build networks, and create a ground swell. It's not something that happens from the top down. It's not something that happens following normal or generally accepted process and procedures.

That's the intention behind The Grassroots Principle. This principle states: Organizations are simply groups of people. Organizations working together means people working together. This happens by creating one relationship at time. THEREFORE, *put effort into building relationships with leaders in other departments*. When you follow the Grassroots Principle, you will

- Identify which organizations with whom to collaborate
- Find an initial point of contact in the organization to build a relationship
- Find a project on which to work that is valuable to both of you.

If this sounds familiar, it should. It's exactly what your SEs and AEs are doing with prospects. You're going to take the same principles you use to sell to external customers and turn them inward. And if this thought bothers you – having to sell collaboration internally –

that is understandable. It used to bother me. I could never understand why this wasn't just natural. You're all part of the same company. You all want the same things. That should allow me to short circuit the whole selling-you-on-an-idea and go right to the getting-it-done. But it doesn't. Human behavior doesn't change, no matter which side of the company line you're on.

You need to accept the fact that most people won't help you simply for the good of company. And it's not written into their job description. You'll need to sell them on the idea. You'll need to get to know them and build their trust. You need to show them what value they'll get from the effort. Then you'll be able to move forward.

Basic Approach

As you think about which organizations with whom to partner and which people to approach, start by understanding "what is on their whiteboard." I use that phrase to indicate the items that are important to the department AND to the individual. I'm sure you get the analogy. When I worked in an office, everyone had their "important stuff" on their whiteboard. There was always a part of it with a border drawn around it, and the words "DO NOT ERASE" near it. That's what you need to have in mind. Those are the areas to which you want your joint effort to somehow contribute. If you can help someone with them, you'll create a valuable internal partnership.

You also need to decide who in the organization is approachable. And I don't mean in the general sense. There will invariably be someone with whom you have some chemistry, whose personality and traits align well with yours. This will make your initial collaboration easier. This person can be your "champion" to the rest of their organization. Once you have that person in mind, look past what they're tasked with achieving in their job and look as well into what they want to accomplish personally. In addition to having chemistry, find someone who has some ambition. Someone looking simply to get done only what's necessary won't likely help when you ask them to work together on something outside of their job description.

Next, decide for which SEs on the team you will Advocate. You'll need to build the relationship to get the work going. Once it is started, you'll want to involve SEs you know will carry that positive momentum forward. Not everyone on your team may be ready to do that. You'll want someone who can manage the additional activity without having it impact their selling, and someone who has something to offer the group with whom they would work. In some cases, this may be someone with some tenure that can talk in depth about selling and the market. Or it may also be someone who perhaps recently joined from a competitor or "in role" position and has a fresh perspective.

Deciding what to do will be driven by the needs of your team. As you will most likely always have a list of things, it's a good idea to pick something that balances a fast win with a significant impact. You'll want something that can be accomplished in weeks, not months. And something that can be used either by a segment of the sales team to help them sell or contributes to a larger marketing, product, or customer success effort. It's easy to get excited about something and follow that excitement only to fall into the trap of having it accomplish something that provides little value or impact.

As your SEs work on this activity, it will be important for you to advertise that work when it makes sense. A key to the Advocate practice is *"PUBLICLY recommend or support"*. As work is accomplished or used in the field, make sure you communicate the value to your management and the rest of the company where it makes sense. Involve others so that they get the value as well and spread the word. This gives your SEs the visibility and recognition intended. In addition, other areas will see the value of collaborating with your team. It will lead to more good opportunities for other SEs to collaborate with other departments.

Now let's take this idea and apply it to how you specifically target and approach other departments. I'll review approaches and collaboration with product marketing, customer success, technical support, and engineering. For each department, we'll look at

- What they care about
- Who you should approach,
- What the SE team can do for them
- What they can do for the SE team
- Suggested initial collaborative projects to build the relationship and provide opportunities to Advocate for your SEs.

Product Marketing

I recommend you put product marketing at the top of the list – assuming you have such a team. I will refer to product marketing as the individual or team that is responsible for teaching the company how to sell its solutions. This group is sometimes part of a larger products group that would include product management and report to a VP of Products or Chief Product Officer. Or it may reside inside the marketing organization and have a VP of product marketing that reports to the head of marketing (Chief Marketing Officer). The team is typically organized around the product taxonomy. In larger organizations with a larger solution set, it may also include one or more people who focus on pricing, packaging, and licensing of the solution.

What's On Their Whiteboard

Product marketing's mission is to:

- Determine who the buyer personas are

- Create and maintain profiles that describe those personas
- Understand persona challenges and needs
- Determine how your solutions meet those needs
- Create the messaging around meeting those needs
- Provide the field with the training and collateral to deliver that messaging

It's a lot. Most product marketing organizations have great intentions but are overwhelmed. Which means they are typically happy to accept some help. In addition, their mission directly supports the mission of the SE team – figure out what to say, show, and do to get the technical win and ultimately the deal.

It should be easy to find opportunities for your SE team to work with product marketing and have them contribute in a larger way to the organization. The unfortunate reality is that product marketers may feel threatened if you approach them with the idea that the SE team can help. They may believe you're suggesting they aren't doing a satisfactory job. They also don't typically get the same level of recognition that the SE team does. After all, the SE team closes deals. Product marketing may make a great slide deck from time to time or deliver an amazing session at sales kickoff. Most of the time, though, they go underappreciated. So, you may experience reluctance when you approach.

The reluctance can be overcome with trust, and trust is built over time through personal relationships. The head of product marketing is the obvious choice, but you may not be able to get that person's attention. The head of a usually understaffed and over tasked department is trying to juggle a lot. It may be more effective to find the ambitious or hardest working individual contributor on the team. That person will find the opportunity to do some cross-departmental collaboration more appealing, as it becomes an opportunity for them to stand out as well.

I always put effort into having a relationship with the head of product marketing. But in addition to the leader, I sought out the product marketer that was vocal, or created the best slides, or regularly suggested new and innovative messaging. That person is your early adopter – someone willing to try new things just for the sake of doing something different. That person will likely be willing to jump into a joint effort with the SE team.

How the SE Team Can Engage

Here are some suggested projects that address items on the product marketing whiteboard where an SE can make a notable contribution:

- Recording demos for both internal and external consumption
- Providing product demonstrations for sales enablement meetings
- Assisting in Persona identification and definition
- Supplying feedback from customers
- Supplying feedback on messaging from competition

These things don't happen often enough. There are several activities you can initiate as the SE leader to make the above contributions and Advocate for your SE team. They are:

Field Advisory Board Meetings

At least once a year, but better every quarter, host a meeting between the SE organization and product marketing team. Where possible, do this meeting in person and add a social aspect to it. Host these at sales kickoff when it's possible to have the product marketing team present. Create a more social atmosphere with drinks and snacks. Make the first 30 minutes just networking and conversation. Follow a basic agenda. Have one of your SEs supply high level information, collected beforehand, about what the SE team accomplished in the previous quarter or year. Have other selected members of the team talk about specific deals, what messaging worked well, what didn't, and what new changes they were seeing in the market – either in prospect needs or competitor motion. Invite the product marketing team to talk about what they accomplished and what their planned activities are for the coming quarter.

One of the byproducts of these meetings is the various SE – product marketer relationships that develop. This leads to lots of good ad hoc collaboration throughout the year. If a product marketer wants some feedback on some new messaging or collateral, they will be comfortable reaching out to the SEs with whom they connected at these meetings. Likewise, if an SE needs something special for a deal, they wouldn't hesitate to reach out to the product marketer with whom they shared a drink and a laugh.

These meetings can still be effective if held remotely. The key is to provide opportunities for as many SEs and product marketers to participate as possible. It's not effective if the combined teams simply listen to their respective leader talk.

Product Marketing Ambassador

This won't create a compelling event. It's more an offering on your part. You'll find your top performers who desire to do more and know how to make bandwidth for special projects. This is an opportunity to name an SE Ambassador to product marketing. This SE's mission is to function as an official conduit between the two teams. Have this SE report out monthly on what they learn from product marketing. Ask them to help with work where possible. When the product marketing team is looking for feedback, help with a demo, someone to present at a webinar, it's the job of the Ambassador to either fulfill the ask or find an SE who can. This is a great opportunity for an SE interested in managing to take on some low-risk management responsibilities. An ambitious SE will take advantage of this and make a significant positive impact with it.

What The SE Team Can Get

Collaborating with the product marketing team also provides you some goodwill you can use later. There will come a time when you'll need their help. You'll have a complicated deal in which you'll need something more than your standard messaging. You'll need to develop collateral or visual aids to clearly differentiate from your competition and get this prospect's attention. This is where you can call in that goodwill and get some cool stuff created.

A highly collaborative relationship with product marketing can be significantly beneficial to the SE team. Because of that, it provides you with an amazing opportunity to Advocate for one or more of your SEs.

Customer Success

The relationship between the SE and customer success teams is also natural, but the opportunities for Advocacy are different. Hopefully, it's not too controversial to say that Customer Success needs the SEs more than the other way around. For this section, I will focus on the part of customer success that is concerned with customer adoption and renewal. Very often tech organizations make professional services and technical support also a part of the larger customer success organization under a Chief Customer Officer. But as it relates to the SE team, the relationship and opportunities for advocacy are quite different with these other two teams.

Not every tech organization has a customer success management team. In those that do, the Customer Success Manager (CSM) is responsible for influencing adoption and renewal in the larger customers. They usually cannot help a customer with use of the product or provide a product demonstration to a group of potential new users. That's where they'll need SE help. This kind of activity would fall to the SE that supported the original purchase. This is a natural motion and doesn't really provide you the opportunity to Advocate. Other situations will arise that will provide such opportunities.

What's On Their Whiteboard

The top priority of the CSM team is to prevent churn. And they'll experience some serious challenges in at risk customers. Challenges for which they may not be as well-equipped as the SE team. These will be customers that need to be resold but have working knowledge of the solution and an unfavorable viewpoint. Most CSMs aren't equipped to sell, let alone sell into that kind of hostile situation. What they will be able to do, and I've found are quite good at, is marshal additional help and resources when needed. While the SE does what she is good at, the CSM will drive the effort and reach out to any other group whose support may be needed. The SE alone would not be sufficient. It takes both field people working together.

Their second priority is to expand a customer's usage. That very often requires the need to sell as well, even though the customer already owns it. I'm sure it's no surprise. Different groups will have different use cases. Depending on how much traction the solution has with the customer, this may even be like a brand-new sale involving additional capability for which the first group wasn't interested. In this case, the CSM typically involves the original salesperson. The SE jumps in like it's a new deal, with the benefit of needing less discovery and hopefully having a more favorable group to which to sell.

Engaging in churn prevention is considered a secondary activity by most SEs and SE Leaders. Renewal dollars aren't typically part of the SE comp plan, so the time spent in renewal is time taken away from selling. Expansion is better but still not considered primary. Despite that outlook, I've come to believe that sales engineers are essential to preventing churn and driving expansion. And while it may never be recognized as an official activity, the SEs still need to be involved. As their efforts may not be monetarily rewarded, this can become an opportunity to Advocate.

How the SE Team Can Engage

Doing it properly means the SE leader has a good working relationship with the CSM Manager. I'll confess that it has not always been easy for me, and it's been more my issue than theirs. When I was an SE, I looked down on the CSMs. Because they generally aren't technical and aren't product experts, most SEs think they can do the CSM job better than the CSMs. What they don't consider is the amount of juggling and coordinating a CSM does. While SEs pride themselves on managing 5-10 open opportunities simultaneously, CSMs often manage 30-40 separate customers at the same time. Even if they could help their customers with product issues, they simply wouldn't have the bandwidth to do it. What they do is develop some amazingly strong relationships by making sure a customer's needs are consistently addressed. Putting aside my preconceived notions was an important first step and may be an important one for you.

Once you've done that, you'll probably find the CSM leader may be the easiest of the leaders to connect with. He knows he needs you and helping him feel like he's a valued working partner will go a long way.

Also, putting some thought and organization around how the SE team supports the CSMs will be important. Things to consider:

- You may need to run interference with sales management. Convincing them that this won't interfere with delivering new business is generally enough. In some cases, AEs are incented on renewal as well, so there is less to worry about.
- It does NOT make sense to dedicate an SE to renewals or designate one or more SEs as go-to. It will be easier from a

workload perspective to assign as it comes. AND it's good for many SEs to get exposed to what customers are doing with the software. They'll gain stories to use with their prospects. They'll develop a better appreciation for what they should position – what is realistic and what is "demo speak." This experience will make them better SEs.

- Make sure you recognize and call it out. An SE that helps save a customer from churning deserves a public nod.

In the end, a healthy working relationship between the SE and CSM team provides not only an opportunity to Advocate for your SEs, but it also provides a superior customer experience.

Technical Support

Though often now considered part of customer success, I believe the opportunities for Advocacy with the tech support team are different than those with the CSMs. I believe there is a kinship of a sorts between support and the SEs. Both teams tend to see a side of the product that the rest of the company does not. SEs need to be creative when they talk to prospects about what's possible. How the solution gets applied is often more important than the solution's documented capability. SEs learn when to say "well, you could use our solution like this...." in a situation where prospects are looking for some way to use a solution outside of its primary function. In the same way – almost mirror like – tech support sees how customers themselves try to use the solution. In doing so, they often meet unknown or unthought of barriers. Support Engineers need to translate what a customer wants to do with how they've tried to use the product and determine if what they want is possible. Much like sales engineers.

Even though tech support is typically not involved in a sales cycle, you have a cousin organization to whom you can extend the value of the SE organization and who, in turn, may above any of the other groups we mention bring value to the SE team.

What's On Their Whiteboard

The highest priority for tech support team is the timely resolution of all customer related issues. In terms of metrics, which translates into support ticket closure rate and the average amount of time a support ticket is open. Most of the time, tech support can manage these on their own. However, situations arise when multiple issues or a regular occurrence of issues causes a customer to want more than just a resolved ticket. And in some cases, there is a breakdown in communication between support and the customer. You've probably encountered this as well. A customer may even have contacted the AE with whom they worked to get help. The AE in turn contacted you to get your assistance.

This is an excellent opportunity to engage with tech support and provide an SE from your team the opportunity to bring their value to the situation. When a support case has taken a long time or many support tickets are open for a given customer, frustration on the customer side prevents them from openly communicating with the support person. This frustration can exist on the support side as well. SEs can be excellent moderators, as they understand the solution and its applications. They are used to dealing with customers, so have the experience to bridge the gap that exists and may continue to grow.

This, however, is unfortunately not activity for which an SE is paid. SEs also tend to be resentful in having to engage in non-deal related stuff. I submit that this is another opportunity for SEs to get an understanding of how the solution they sell is used and what limitations it may be experiencing. Or what misunderstandings exist within customers about what a solution can do. I believe that SEs don't want to find themselves selling a solution for a use case for which it isn't suited. By being exposed to what customers are doing and what problems they encounter, SEs can experience this firsthand. In addition, they can use their selling skills to delight a customer once again and resolve an unfortunate situation.

Bottom line: don't hesitate to get an SE involved in helping tech support resolve a particularly difficult customer issue or deal with a difficult customer situation. The SE is very often exactly what's needed, and they'll gain experience that benefits them going forward. I would even suggest that, where possible, arrange to have SEs spend regular time resolving support tickets. Where you have the reasonable means to allow your SEs to rotate out of the field, even for an hour or two, and help support in responding to requests from customers. This experience will help round the SEs knowledge of the solution and understand what customers struggle with. It will give them the opportunity to stretch beyond their normal routine and bring value to an organization that, like the other teams we've mentioned, has more to do than their staff can manage.

Products / Engineering

If what you sell is more on the technical side and being sold to a technical audience, this group rather than product marketing is probably your top priority to connect with to provide opportunities to Advocate for your team. And I would bet there's a good chance your SEs are already taking the initiative to connect with people in engineering and / or products.

But Advocate is about you getting the SEs that don't have those connections the same opportunities and on a bigger stage. That starts with you making connections yourself. If you aren't connected to engineering or products, that is your first move. In some cases, these are different organizations, and in others, product management and engineering are together. Engineering will most likely have greater value to your SE team, especially if your product is highly technical or sold to a technical audience. Getting someone who is responsible for code can help you quickly deal with product issues during a POC or get you access to alpha or beta versions in those selling situations when a forward look helps get a deal done.

What's On Their Whiteboard

It's up to this department to create, maintain, and enhance the technical product you're selling. If it's software, they're writing code. If it's a device, they build prototypes, confirm their viability, and then figure out how to mass produce them. In some cases, the sales engineer is an integral part of this because the products you create are built custom for the specific customer. Whatever the situation, you and your team make your living selling what this team creates. It's only natural that you can find ways to plug your SEs into this team.

If we break down further what's on this team's whiteboard, you'll find some obvious opportunities to showcase an SE. Creating the product starts with understanding the challenges potential customers face. If you have a product management team, this is their job. What's ironic is that most product management teams don't spend too much time – or any time at all – in front of customers. They interface with analysts and do research. They then translate that information into product requirements, then collaborate with the developers or engineers as they build. Engineers spend even less time in front of customers. They are generally only involved when there are catastrophic product issues with a specific customer. Otherwise, they are heads down writing code. If your development team follows any kind of agile creation process, they will work in sprints, which is a time bound period of creation. During those sprints, they probably do a daily 15 minute stand up meeting to each talk about what piece of work they will do that day.

At some point, with a critical mass of features being nearly created, they will start talking about a release – which basically means they provide the newly created capabilities to existing customers and make them available for you and your team to sell. There is also typically a frenzy of activity from marketing as this is an excellent reason to get in front of the market again.

How Can the SE Team Help

Finding opportunities to advocate for your team means figuring out how you help the product and engineering team throughout this process. The first and most obvious should jump out at you. They spend no time in front of actual customers. You do. While product managers may feel threatened by you sharing your customer facing experience (after all, this is their value to the company to be the voice of the market), most engineers will love it. Consider that most engineers share similar personality traits: introverted, intellectual, geeky. It's an entire subculture that while currently enjoying popularity still shies away from human interaction. But every developer wants to know what users think of what they've created. And since they don't get customer facing time, this is your opportunity to provide that perspective. Here are several suggestions from my past, where I have been successful in Advocating for SEs with the product and engineering team.

Run a regular Field Advisory Board meeting. As mentioned with product marketing, this team would also most likely welcome dedicated time to hear from the field. This doesn't need to be long or drawn out - and doesn't necessarily need to be live either. Delegate one of your SEs to gather feedback from the rest of the team about what they heard from customers and prospects over the last quarter. Have them consolidate it and make it presentable. Use the same format for every meeting to make it easier to communicate. Then schedule a meeting and invite your engineering team to take part. You'll need to work with engineering and product management to decide who that should be. Of course, record the meeting and make it available to everyone to watch. Promote that video internally as well.

Conduct Proof of Value / Trial postmortem review meetings. If a proof of value or proof of concept or trial is a regular part of your sales cycle, give the product team insight into how those are executed. I used a standard form that included basic information about the customer and the deal, the success criteria for the activity and then a breakdown of what went well and what could have been better from both the product and team perspective. I would then ask the lead SE to schedule a 30-minute meeting to review that information with product and engineering leads. I would also ask that SE to record the meeting to make it available to everyone.

Volunteer to provide QA and User Acceptance testing prior to a major release. For software companies, everyone knows there is never enough testing performed before releasing new features to the market. User acceptance testing is difficult to coordinate because you want to involve actual users, which is difficult to do. Fortunately, the SE team can play the role of a user very well – and is much easier to coordinate with. Provide some folks from your team to play that part. This is the perfect job for newer SEs who are up to speed on the product but may not have a lot of activity in the field yet. It gives them the opportunity to be hugely useful and gives them access to the new stuff. They can help the dev team, and you can have them report back to the rest of the SE team on what's coming.

Help with a product Beta program. Like QA testing, most software shops would ideally like to have some extended use time with select customers before making the new stuff generally available. Organizing and managing a Beta program is a lot of coordination. Customer success typically takes the lead with this, but they can always use help. They need to identify customers willing to commit to using the beta version for a short period of time and to then provide feedback. Your SE team will typically still have relationships with the people to whom they've sold. They can help the CS team solicit those volunteers and gather feedback during the program. And if the CS team isn't running a Beta program, this is something for you to consider. As stated, it takes some serious coordination, but also provides some serious benefits.

As a final thought: don't underestimate the influence you and the SE team have over the direction of the product. While you may believe that the rest of the company views you as the "demo team," they also know well that product doesn't get sold without you. And while the engineers especially have a large sense of pride and in some cases arrogance, they (perhaps more than the SEs) crave the positive feedback that comes from a happy and delighted user. Use that need. Be the voice of the market to the engineering team. The SEs, more than anyone else in the company, understand and identify with the engineers. Use that compatibility to give your SEs the opportunity to provide their input and participate in this part of the company.

Conclusion

Being recognized, having the opportunity to share their creativity, being promoted on a larger stage – these are all part of your SE team's hierarchy of needs. For you to be successful with this, you need to create and keep relationships with other related functions: product marketing, customer success, technical support, products & engineering. By having good working relationships with the leadership in these various groups, you'll make it possible for you to Advocate for your SEs by giving them cross-department collaboration projects. It should be something you make part of your regular routine and not simply leave to time and random, ad hoc opportunity. It's part of your responsibility to the SEs that work for you to give them these opportunities, and you'll find you will benefit in terms of job satisfaction and career opportunity.

7: Aspire

The word Aspire means *to direct one's hopes or ambitions towards achieving something*. We all aspire to something. And then most of us spend 90,000 hours or more working over the period of our lifetime. 90,000 hours. It's a huge investment of time. And in that time, we hope to either be able to directly achieve those aspirations in our work or produce the funds necessary to achieve some of those aspirations. It's the "why we do it."

I certainly aspired to things when I graduated university and began my career. At that point, they were simple. Get a job. Save for retirement. Get married, have a family. I took a corporate job with a Fortune 10 company and thought – this is it. Job done. But while working, I encountered people – managers and leaders – who were able to help me aspire to more. Through such leadership and influence, I struck out on my own for the first time. When that didn't work, it was other influence that helped me get my first sales engineer job, and through that realize that I could aspire for even more. Another leader helped me see my potential for leadership, which led to executive level roles.

When I started working, I had no such aspirations. It was only through the guidance of caring leaders that I was able to see that I was capable of more. I believe I'm not alone in this. Most people don't have the ability to see their own potential. We point to those that do and wish we could be like them. And yes, there are a few – the outliers – who see and believe deeply in their own abilities. And as a result, they achieve that for which they are capable. But most people need help doing this. That's where you, the SE Manager, play your part. You look at your SEs from the outside. You'll see in them what they're capable of differently then they will. In many cases, they will not realize their own potential. It will take your coaching and guidance to build their confidence and allow them to see the possibilities. In other cases, they will be overanxious or have the desire to do something for which they aren't especially a fit. While a `more difficult conversation, it's still your responsibility to be honest in this situation as well. And that isn't about discouraging so much as it is redirecting to something for which` they are better suited.

By way of example: when I ran a presales team in EMEA, there were two technical solutions engineers (TSE) with about the same tenure, both of whom indicated they wanted to be promoted to Solutions Consultants. The TSE team was invaluable to sales as they did much of the technical heavy lifting in a POC, managed the demo environment, and provided the SC team some deeper product expertise. No one we hired into this role, though, wanted to stay in the role. Every TSE aspired to be a solutions consultant – in front of customers, working with sales, closing deals. The EMEA division of the company had a very sales focused culture. SCs were given lots of recognition and glory. TSEs not as much. Both people were excellent TSEs, but in quite different ways. One of them was very meticulous. He loved doing configuration work in the product. He was an artist, creating amazing interface and analytics for proof of value activities. Prospects absolutely loved the things he created. He put enough time and effort into the proof exercise that his work could be used by the customer in production once they purchased. The AEs weren't so excited about this, as it tended to extend the sales cycle. The other TSE was very *deal* oriented. He wanted to be involved in the selling process as much as possible. He worked with a sense of urgency and built only what was necessary to get the deal done. And the AEs appreciated and trusted him more. While both wanted to be SCs, I knew one would clearly work better with the AEs in the field than the other. I promoted the deal-oriented TSE. That TSE went on to become a successful AE himself. The other was initially bitter and ended up leaving. He became an independent consultant doing configuration work in the product for existing customers – and never looked back. He later admitted to me that while not getting promoted stung, it was better for him overall as he feels he is happier doing the consulting work as opposed to being an SC. In fact, when I had an SC opening and asked him about it, he indicated that he knew now that wasn't what he wanted to do.

The Three Perceptions

In the story above, there was a clear next step for one of the Technical Solutions Engineers. Continuing with the story, that person once promoted to SC was later promoted to Senior SC. Once he achieved that promotion, after a time he indicated a desire to transition to sales. This is where things became more challenging. And typically, where SEs run into obstacles.

The pure sales engineer career path tends to be short. There are typically 2-3 levels of that role. Your next step within the profession is to be promoted to management. The path narrows very quickly at that point, so many SEs feel stuck. As a result, after spending some time at one company, they look to another company and start the process over again – this time with the hope that they'll have better opportunities.

It doesn't have to be this way. The reality is that anyone with experience as a sales engineer has a unique set of experiences and perspective on the company. They are in sales, so they are an integral part of acquiring revenue and growing the business. They learn how to talk about the business value of their technical product to other business leaders. They are also technical, which means they understand the product and how it works. Many also get involved with customers after the sale, so they are familiar with how the product gets used. They experience firsthand that what the customer asked for prior to purchasing changes once they realize what is possible, they also know that most customers will never implement the "art of the possible" from their first demo, and usually only end up using a small amount of the product's full capability. Many get some experience collaborating with the Products team, so they have an understanding how the product is made. They may also get involved helping marketing create messaging and promote a new release. In summary, they pretty much see the entire business lifecycle end to end. They may never go deep in any one specific area, but their broad experience makes them good candidates for many of these other roles.

But they are rarely looked at that way. Why?? There are reasons, most of which are based on three skewed perceptions and less on actual working knowledge.

Perception One

Some consider that being able to provide a product demo doesn't equate to knowing what it takes for a customer to successfully use the product. They believe there is a distinct division between those who sell the product and those who implement it. Most sales engineers know that this division is extremely blurry. While it's true that the SE is less involved once the sale is done, it does not mean they are not exposed. It also does not mean that some strange and completely different thing happens with the product once the sale is completed. This is just a perception, but one that seems ingrained especially in higher management.

Perception Two

Many business leaders worry about having the best SEs move out of the field. They don't want anything to disrupt revenue generation. But given that the best SEs are usually the most ambitious, those SEs at some point will want the next role, the next challenge, the next move up. They will, like in my example, want to move into sales or products or management, or on to another company where they believe they may have a better chance at management. Meaning, the thing those leaders fear is likely to happen anyway. The root of the perception is many believe good SEs are impossible to find. Once you have one, you need to keep them in place at all costs. This is the second perception which you will need to overcome.

Perception Three

Finally, many find that because an SE doesn't have direct experience in a different role, that makes them less capable or even incapable of being successful in that role - or at least too much of a risk to consider. They feel like they'll be getting less than an entry level candidate when, ideally, they are hoping to hire someone with experience. They don't see the perspective that an SE has on the business, one that extends well beyond sales. They also don't realize the mix of skills an SE possess to be successful in the role. This is the third perception you will need to overcome.

It's a tragedy for a company to lose the talent it has in its best SEs if those SEs want to progress but have nowhere else to go. Some SEs will be content to do what they do for a while. But that will not be the majority. After some time, maybe a few years, maybe less, the best SEs will want their next role. It will most likely NOT be your role. What will you do?

The SE Career Path

To serve your SEs and help them achieve what they aspire to will require you to do two things:

1. Forge the career path. Overcome the three perceptions that prevent SEs from moving into other roles. That means connecting with the managers in those other areas to understand what it would take and put the possibilities in place
2. Make sure that the SE is ready when you have the path created. The best way to do this is to establish a regular Talent Management cadence from the beginning – one that includes regular feedback, coaching, and quarterly goal setting.

To finish that story: the person that went from technical solutions engineer to solutions consultant and then wanted to move into sales got his wish. The move to sales was not automatic. Of all the moves an SE makes, this is probably the most common. But most sales leaders realize the transition isn't easy. Not everyone can make it or should. Fortunately, this person established himself as a sales-oriented SE. He worked on and was able to emphasize his sales acumen. He created great relationships with the sales team and regional leader. And finally, he and I worked with the regional sales lead to put a transition plan in place. It consisted of me finding someone to replace him, so we didn't lose capacity, as well as coaching him to be ready for the sales role. He made his number his first year and has continued to be successful ever since.

Establish a Talent Management Cadence

Talent management is not a new practice. In simple terms, it's the methodology you use to find the right people to hire, onboard them, and develop them to do great things for your company. We covered the hiring part in Augment. I want to take it the rest of the way here.

As we've already established, the role of sales engineer is unique. The people that take it on are unique. Every HR department has the right intentions, but what your company typically provides for talent management won't suffice for the SE team. Just like you need to Activate the working environment so that SEs can thrive, you need to tune your talent management practices so they're most effective for your SE team. What follows is an overview of what I have successfully used in the past. I offer it as a guide. I'll highlight what I believe were the critical elements. What's important is not that you follow step-by-step what I've done, but that you adopt a methodology that helps you develop your SEs and prepare them for their next move – whatever that is and whenever it comes.

Track Their Capabilities

This starts first with creating an SE Capability Matrix. Use the Service Catalog and KSET profile as starting points. You want to assess what services your SEs can deliver and how well they deliver them. You also want to understand how well each currently aligns to the profile of the A Player and where they could improve.

I also apply the Intuition Principle mentioned earlier. It's not enough to simply think or hope that an SE "gets it." This isn't a yes or no to both questions. Your Capability Matrix should outline the specifics of what an SE needs to know and to deliver and then should provide some quantitative measure of their ability. That quantitative measure should be from either data you collect or by a rating you assign. Start by creating table arranged like this:

		Activity Tracking			Service Delivery		KST Profile Ratings			
Name	OTE	Deal Contributions	POC Success Rate	# Deals Touched	Demo Capability	POC Capability	Domain	Product	Selling	Individual

Figure 7: SE Capability Matrix Framework

You'll see the table combines comp and activity information with what an SE can deliver and how well they align to the A Player profile. Adding comp and activity will help you quickly spot an SE that is underpaid (and at risk of leaving) or someone who isn't operating to the level you need.

To get more specific and practical, here's an example. I used to use a multi-tab Excel spreadsheet as my first Capability Matrix. For the Service Delivery section, I had five columns for each product or set of products in the portfolio. Those were:

- **RFx**: meaning the SE knew enough about the product to respond to an RFP about it
- **Preso:** The SE could provide a presentation on the product, but not necessarily a product demonstration. Given that the portfolio was big, this helped prevent having to bring 2-3 SEs on a sales call. In some cases, being able to present and talk about what a product could do was good enough.
- **OOB**: The SE could deliver the standard demonstration and tailor the base demo story for a given prospect.
- **Config**: The SE could configure the product to provide a demo that would address a prospect's specific challenges.

- **POC**: The SE could deploy the product in a customer environment and supporting a proof of concept or trial.

I would put an x in the cell in that column if the SE could deliver the service, confirmed by the manager or me. In addition, I assigned points to the various services – 1 point for RFX, 2 for Preso, and so on. This allowed me to set a minimum score that an SE or an entire team needed to have. I could quickly see where we needed to do more enablement and which SEs needed it.

Solution Architect	Current Role (SC/TC)	Product One						Product Two					
East Region Team		RFX	Preso	OOB	CFG	POC	Score	RFx	Preso	OOB	CFG	POC	Score
SC Name 1	SC						0						0
SC Name 2	SC	x	x	x	x	x	15	x	x	x	x	x	15
TC Name 1	TC						0	x					1
SC Name 3	SC	x	x	x	x	x	15	x	x	x	x	x	15
TC Name 2	TC		x				2	x	x				3
SC Name 4	SC	x	x	x	x	x	15	x	x	x	x	x	15
TC Name 5	TC		x				2	x	x				3
East Team Average		3	5	3	3	3	7	6	5	3	3	3	7.42857

Figure 8: Sample SE Capability Matrix

You'll notice we use the title Solution Architect instead of SE, and there were two types: Technical Consultants and Solution Consultants. It was not uncommon for someone who was a Technical Consultant to want to move into a Solution Consultant role. The expectation was that a TC would do RFP responses and help on POCs but not any of the presentation work. Using the Capability Matrix, I would help a particular TC build on what she already knew. Looking at the above table at TC Name1, I can see she has started with Product Two. I would help her build on that knowledge by first coaching her on how to present the product. Once she was able to successfully present and message, I would then help her with the demo. When she had a check in Preso and OOB, meaning she could present and demonstrate the basic product, I would consider her ready to be promoted to the first level of SC.

Assess Their Potential

In addition to a quantitative measure of their profile and ability to deliver, you want to have some outlook on their potential, considering what they may want to do next. In Talent Management, a 9-box grid is often used. According to modern business legend, it has its origins when consulting firm McKinsey created it for General Electric to use to assess business investments. The grid was formed from two axis – one a measure of potential, the other a measure of performance. That square was then subdivided into three parts on each side, forming the 9 boxes. The top right was the best place to be, bottom left the worst. Then some smart HR people saw that and adapted it for use with talent management, to classify people based on their potential and performance.

I first encountered this at HP, with the 9 boxes being reduced to 4 (apparently not uncommon). The horizontal or x axis was "promotability", the potential equivalent, and the vertical axis was performance. What appealed to me about it was the upper left quadrant – the high performer low promotability person. I found this appealing because I had many solution consultants on my team that I felt fit this category. They didn't want management roles, and most would not have been suited for them anyway. They didn't necessarily want to take roles in different teams. But we needed a way to promote them. At the time, HP had the concept of a Principal and a Fellow. In these roles, someone wouldn't manage people, but they were recognized as both an industry expert and subject matter expert with one or more parts of the software portfolio. I thought this was brilliant. Now I had an additional career path to offer SEs that wanted to stay in the team but didn't want to manage.

When I moved on, I brought this Talent Grid with me. It was the tool I used to help set coaching objectives for every individual as well as have an overall view of the team.

The grid looked like this:

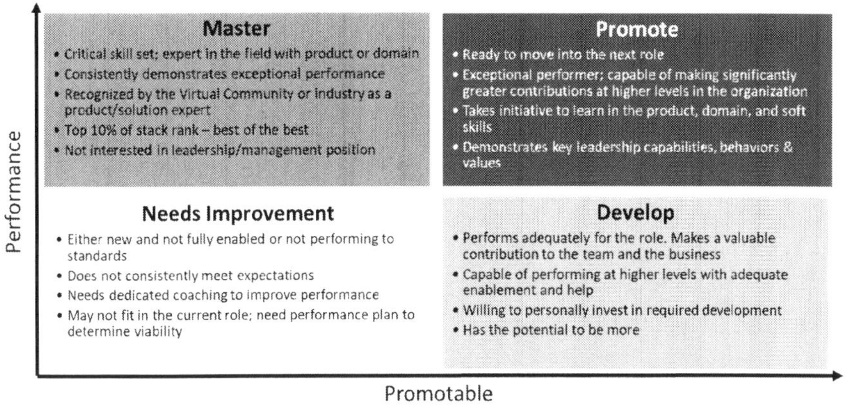

Figure 9: Basic Talent Grid

Every quarter, I would determine in which box each of the SEs belonged. I had a PowerPoint deck that I copied and updated by placing their name in the appropriate quadrant. On the diagram of the grid, you can see the definitions for each one. I also used these basic guidelines.

Needs Improvement

Every *new* SE belongs in Needs Improvement. That was just a fact of their newness and not a reflection of my doubt in their ability. Every SE in the Needs Improvement quadrant required a specific and individual improvement plan whose objective was to have that SE out of the Needs Improvement box by the end of the quarter. The "improvement plan" for your new SEs should just be the usual onboarding plan. What you provide any other SE in this quadrant should be specific to improving them so they can continue to be a contributing member of the team.

I'll confess I didn't always believe this. I felt it was my responsibility to manage out anyone who didn't perform well. I often heard the phrase "fail fast" from other managers. My justification was that by letting a low performer go, I was freeing them up to find a role that was better suited for them. What I didn't think then, but believe now, is that it was *MY responsibility to help them find that next role if they weren't going to be successful on my team*. Everyone has something good to offer in some role. My job as their manager is to uncover what that is and put it where it will do its best.

I say this to encourage you to do the same. It's true that you may find that not everyone you have on your team belongs there. You may have inherited them. Or you may have misjudged when you hire them. They may have changed over time. Whatever the reason, they are on your team now. If you don't believe they can perform to the required level or they no longer have that desire, spend the time working to find the place where they do belong.

Develop and Master

The Develop quadrant is most likely where most of your team will be. For everyone here, you should have an end goal of determining if they want to move to Master or Promote. They may not, and that's fine as well. There is no time limit for someone in Develop other than their own career desires. For a future Master, you'll be working to get them recognition not just in the broader company but in the industry as well. This is where your practice advocating for them will come in. Your company's marketing department should be a great vehicle to get these SEs the opportunity to be with analysts, speak at conferences, author whitepapers, and just generally get broader exposure. Anyone in the Master quadrant stays in your SE team.

Promote

The SEs looking to be managers or move to another role are basically looking to move out of your team. These are the SEs you are working toward the Promote box. Think of Promote not just as the box for management candidates, but for any SE you would "promote" as being a good fit for another team. That might be product management, product marketing, sales – whatever. The development plan you create for them is more about doing the things they need to prepare them for the new role, not anything that necessarily makes them a better SE. You'll need to work with management in the other departments to identify what those things are and probably get help in coaching the SE on them.

Please don't be one of those managers who discourages anyone leaving your team. Leaving is a natural consequence of good talent management. Your challenge will be to decide how best to help someone prepare for a roll in which you may have no experience. You'll also need to then go hire a replacement for that person. But you'll have created a tremendous amount of good will and built your reputation as a caring people manager. This person will carry a positive outlook about you to their next team. The other SEs in your team will see your selfless effort and be more appreciative and loyal for it.

It's also important to reaffirm to those SEs that their development work doesn't guarantee them a role someplace else. This is of course where things become a bit tricky, and your honesty is essential. The best you can offer is that you work with the other leadership to prepare the SE. You also encourage that SE to reach out to that leader and develop a relationship on their own. You counsel that SE to have patience. The team they want to join may not need anyone. The business may not be ready to expand. It may put that SE's resolve to the test, waiting to take that next role, which isn't a bad thing.

There are logistics you'll need to consider when helping an SE move to a different role as well, most notably with Human Resources. It's fair to say that SE compensation is at the higher end when compared to other roles. You'll need to prepare the SE for this, which is probably the easier part. The SE that wants to move to products or customer success or delivery isn't motivated by money. If they were, they would stay SEs. Your HR business partner will have a more challenging time with it. HR finds it difficult to accept that someone would take what they consider a step backwards in pay. Now, I realize I am making a large generalization. In my experience, this has been true. I point this out to encourage you to take time to work with HR. You may also need to push a little. You'll find yourself being an intermediary between the SE that wants to move, their intended new leader, and the HR department. That's where you should be. The work you do here will help forge the path for other SEs that want to make the same move – if that work hasn't already been done.

The Quarterly Coaching Plan

Use the Capability Matrix and Talent Grid as tools to support a quarterly coaching process. Start the quarter by updating both tools for every SE on the team. If you have managers and directors reporting to you, ask them to do it for their teams. Based on each SE's position in the Talent Grid and their desire and capabilities, determine what to coach them on that will have the most impact for them. For SEs in the Needs Improvement and Develop grids, the Capability Matrix will point you to what knowledge or skills they need and which services they need to learn to deliver. If you want to move them to Expert or Promote, you'll need to look outside the capability matrix to get them what they need.

The plan itself shouldn't ask them to achieve more than three outcomes, depending of course on the size of the outcome. One may be fine. Make the outcome as specific as possible (SE certified on ability to demo Product A). Determine milestones to track through the quarter that will lead to that goal (SE completes product training course, SE learns standard demo script, SE shadows others demonstrating that product, etc.) and put timing against those milestones. The format you use isn't necessarily relevant. If your company is using an HR system that allows you to document and track goals and objectives for an individual, it's a good idea to use it.

It IS necessary to document this in some way. You'll need it so you have visibility into everyone's progress. Keep notes and update the coaching plan throughout the quarter. You and your leadership team should be meeting with every individual regularly (say bi-weekly) to track progress, motivate them, or make updates if things change. Then at the end of the quarter, you know what's been achieved and how to update the Capability Matrix and Talent Grid appropriately.

Documenting this kind of development is also important from an HR perspective. If the work a given SE does is significant, you can use this documented effort to justify a mid-cycle increase in their compensation plan or a promotion. It also becomes your insurance policy. If it becomes necessary to let someone go because they choose not to perform to expected standards, the coaching plan documents your efforts to help them. If the company decided it needs to reduce its workforce because of business or economic conditions, the coaching plans outline all the amazing work the SEs are doing in addition to helping drive revenue and may work to help you keep their jobs.

Find Your Successor

In all this Aspiration work, it's important that you identify the person that will eventually take your place. Succession planning is also a core part of any manager's responsibility. I have no specific method or process for this. It wasn't until I was well into my first management role that my current boss indicated that I should work on identifying a successor. It's not typically an immediate or even a quarterly plan. But it is key to you realizing your own aspirations. If those aspirations happen to have you exactly where you want to be for the long term, so be it. But if you're good at leading, there is a fair bet that your company may want to leverage your talent in other places. If you do aspire to other roles or to take larger leadership roles, you won't be able to claim them until your manager and the sales management team you work with are confident you have a viable replacement.

The shortest path is someone from your own team who has leadership potential or aspiration. If someone has potential but hasn't necessarily indicated a desire to manage, it's worth starting that conversation. I didn't ask for my first management role. I was approached by my boss's boss to consider it. I hadn't really thought it a possibility until he approached me. The SE with such potential on your team may have the same perspective. They may just need to be introduced to the idea to warm up to it.

Whatever your situation, identifying someone to take your place is prudent. Call it insurance or risk management or business continuity. You owe it to yourself, to the business, and to your team to make sure someone is there to continue to take care of them.

Conclusion

It's a lot of work. It absolutely is.

There is a significant amount of effort that you'll need to put into this quarterly coaching process. It's easy to get distracted by the deals. I know this may be considered sacrilegious to say. Aren't the deals everything? They aren't if you sacrifice the SE team to get them. All dramatic statements aside – you will need to make the time to do this development. Most likely no one will hold you accountable to doing it or pester you about it. You won't have a sales leader bugging you about why a coaching plan isn't updated like they will about making sure an SE is ready for that critical demo. In fact, you can go a whole quarter and not do any of this, and no one would say anything. Your SEs will go on delivering SE services, and you'll go on doing meeting after meeting. Your day will be full, and you'll feel you're contributing. But it won't be the right work. And when you lose an SE because they left to find the next challenge, that's when you'll regret not putting this effort in. This stuff is that important. This is the regular care and feeding that propels the SE team forward. Don't neglect it or let it be second priority. You won't see immediate results. This is the long game that every good leader plays.

8: The Wrap Up

I hope what I have relayed here will serve you well. I hope it is a source of inspiration to always work your SE management craft. I hope it's understood that they aren't a step-by-step set of instructions. You'll get the most out of them through regular practice and adapting them to the specifics of your situation and style.

In the spirit of developing yourself, I encourage you again to make reading a core part of your self-development and a daily practice. I urge you to connect with other sales engineer leaders to share, discuss, and collaborate on the profession. I think a community can be one of the best sources of knowledge and learning. Remember the proverb from Chapter 3. Don't just join a community. Being active in it will motivate and elevate you.

You may notice that I invested none of the writing to talk about approving travel requests, expense reports, or requests for time off. You must do those things. My learning – do them as quickly as you can and don't neglect them. These are the little things that prove to your team that you care about their careers and not just yours.

Finally, I would love to hear from you if you would be willing to share your thoughts, no matter what they are. If you think this is complete garbage and want to express it, I want to know. If the opposite is true, and there is some way I can help you. Please don't hesitate to respond. You can always reach me at billbalnave@gmail.com, on LinkedIn as long it exists, or in Discord as billbalnave#9451.

Acknowledgements

This is my favorite part of the book. I am proud of myself for completing it, but it is in no way something I achieved alone.

To my mother, from whom I get my drive and work ethic. You taught me constant self-improvement and didn't take any excuses from me. You always wanted more for me, and I love you for that very much.

To my soulmate **Anni Keil**, who was my partner in crime and coach in life long before she became my wife. You always believed in me. You continually encouraged me. You pushed when I needed it. Thanks babe.

To my sons, **Liam** and **Colin Balnave**, who supported a father who traveled a lot while they were growing up without complaint. I would not have had the career experiences I draw on for this book without their support.

To **Kathy Eastwood**, who after lots of loud contentious discussions and drinks has become one of my best and closest friends, a career coach and mentor. You opened my eyes to lots of possibilities and put me back on course on more than one occasion. And you, more than many, helped me author this book. I almost feel like I should include your name on the front you helped so much.

To **David Griffin**, who gave me my first opportunity to lead and continued to challenge me to do more.

To **Mike Fey**, who was a great first boss when I became a first boss. I think my management career would have been much rougher if I had ended up working directly for anyone else.

To **Jack Fine**, who gave me a singular appreciation for the profession and craft of managing people. You may not realize how much you inspired and pushed me, and I didn't express enough how much I appreciated it.

To **Aash Mangrulka**r, who was always willing to debate with me, even if I was clearly out of my mind about something. We could be diametrically opposed but always walk away from the discussion still friends.

To **John Care**, with whom I had the pleasure of developing and delivering some of the most fun SE enablement in my career. I even remember a car ride discussion about evolution vs. design theory that was quite lively!

To **Sunny Gupta** and **Larry Blasko**, who gave me "a seat at the table" and a voice in the business itself.

To **Chris White**, who made me realize that authoring and publishing a book was achievable.

To **Dan Lipson**, who shared his love of SE leadership and was willing to give me honest but edifying feedback on this book. You were extremely thoughtful and helpful and certainly didn't need to invest as much in it as you did. Thanks for the time, Dan!

To **Darren Huggins**, who shares the same passion of SEs and SE management, and whose insight I respect and appreciate tremendously. Thanks, Darren, for giving me some early morning time to read and help shape the book.

And finally, to all the sales engineers, solutions consultants, and solution architects with whom I've had the privilege to work. Thank you for everything I learned from you, and apologies if some of those lessons came at your expense.

Readings That Inspired This Book

The 7 Habits of Highly Effective People by Stephen Covey

The Speed of Trust by Stephen M. R. Covey

Leaders Eat Last by Simon Sinek

Think Different by Adam Grant

Dream Teams by Shane Snow

The Effective Executive by Peter Drucker

Topgrading by Bradford D Smart

The Six Habits of Highly Effective sales engineers by Chris White

Thinking, Fast and Slow by Daniel Kahneman

Flow by Mihaly Csikszentmihalyi

Printed in Great Britain
by Amazon

34070981R00090